How to Form Your Own Corporation

With State-by-State Laws and Forms for Every State

By W. Kelsea Wilber and
Arthur G. Sartorius, III
Attorneys at Law

Sphinx Publishing
Sphinx International, Inc.
1725 Clearwater-Largo Rd., S.
Post Office Box 25
Clearwater, FL 34617
Tel: (813) 587-0999
Fax: (813) 586-5088

Note: The law changes constantly and is subject to different interpretations. It is up to you to check it thoroughly before relying on it. Neither the author nor the publisher guarantees the outcome of the uses to which this material is put.

First edition, 1993

ISBN 0-913825-61-1
Library of Congress Catalog Number: 93-83841

Manufactured in the United States of America.

This publication is designed to provide accurate and authoritative information in regard to the subject matter covered. It is sold with the understanding that the publisher is not engaged in rendering legal, accounting or other professional services. If legal advice or other expert assistance is required, the service of a competent professional person should be sought.

> -From a Declaration of Principles jointly adopted by a Committee of the American Bar Association and a Committee of Publishers.

Published by Sphinx Publishing, a division of Sphinx International, Inc., Post Office Box 25, Clearwater, Florida 34617. Tel. (800) 226-5291. This publication is available by mail for $19.95 plus Florida sales tax if applicable, plus $2.50 shipping.

Table of Contents

Using Self-Help Law Books

Whenever you shop for a product or service you are faced with many different levels of quality and price. In deciding upon which one to buy you make a cost/value analysis based upon your willingness to pay and the quality you desire.

When buying a car you decide whether you want transportation, comfort, status or sex appeal, and you decide among such choices as a Chevette, a Lincoln, a Rolls Royce or a Porsche. Before making a decision you usually weigh the merits of each against the cost.

When you get a headache, you can take a pain reliever such as aspirin or you can go to a medical specialist for a neurological examination. Given this choice most people, of course, take a pain reliever, since it only costs pennies whereas a medical examination would cost hundreds of dollars and take a lot of time. This is usually a very logical choice because very rarely is anything more than a pain reliever needed for a headache. But in some cases a headache may indicate a brain tumor and failing to go to a specialist right away can result in complications. Should everyone with a headache go to a specialist? Of course not, but people treating their own illnesses must realize that they are taking a chance, based upon their cost/value analysis of the situation, that they are choosing the most logical option.

The same cost/value analysis must be made in deciding to do one's own legal work. Many legal situations are very simple, requiring a simple form and no complicated analysis. Anyone with a little intelligence and a book of instructions can handle the matter simply.

But there is always the chance that there is a complication involved which only a lawyer would notice. To simplify the law into a book like this, often several legal cases must be condensed into a single sentence or paragraph. Otherwise, the book would be several hundred pages long and too complicated for most people. However, this simplification necessarily leaves out many details and nuances which would apply to special or unusual situations. Also, there are many ways to interpret most legal questions. Your case may come before a judge who disagrees with the analysis of our author.

Therefore, in deciding to use a self-help law book and in doing your own legal work you must realize that you are making a cost/value analysis and deciding that the chance that your case will not turn out to your satisfaction is outweighed by the money you will save by doing it yourself. Most people doing their own simple legal matters will probably never have a problem. But occasionally someone may find out that it ended up costing them more later to have an attorney straighten out the situation than it would have if they had hired an attorney in the beginning. Keep this in mind while handling your case and be sure to consult an attorney if you feel you might need further guidance.

Another thing to keep in mind is that laws change constantly and it would be impossible for us to know of every change as it occurs and recall every book from every bookstore to replace it. If you file a legal form and it is returned because something new is needed, you will usually be told what is required and will be able to refile your form quickly.

Introduction

Each year hundreds of thousands of corporations are registered in this country and it is not a coincidence that the largest businesses in the world are corporations. The corporation is the preferred method of doing business for most people because it offers many advantages over partnerships and sole proprietorships.

The main reason people incorporate is to avoid personal liability. While sole proprietors and partners have all of their personal assets at risk, corporate shareholders risk only what they paid for their stock. With so many people ready to sue for any reason or for no reason, the corporation is one of the few inexpensive protections left.

Creating a simple corporation is very easy and it is the purpose of this book to explain, in simple language, how you can do it yourself. A simple corporation as used in this book is one in which there are five or fewer shareholders and all of them are active in the business. If you plan to sell stock to someone who is not active in the business or to have six or more shareholders, you should seek the advice of an attorney. However, some guidance is provided throughout this book as to what some of the concerns will be in these circumstances.

If your situation is in any way complicated or involves factors not mentioned in this book, you should seek the advice of an attorney practicing corporate law. The cost of a short consultation can be a lot cheaper than the consequences of violating the law.

If you plan to sell stock to outside investors you should consult with a lawyer who specializes in securities laws. Selling a few thousand shares of stock to friends and neighbors may sound like an easy way to raise capital for your business, but it is not! Since the stock market crash of the 1930s there have been federal laws regulating the sale of securities. There are harsh criminal penalties for violators and the laws don't have many loopholes. The basic rules are explained in Chapter V.

This book also explains the basics of corporate taxation, but you should discuss your own particular situation with your accountant before deciding what is best for you. He or she can also set you up with an efficient system of bookkeeping which can save both time and money.

Good luck with your new business!

Chapter 1
What is a Corporation?

A corporation is a legal "person" which can be created under state law. As a person, a corporation has certain rights and obligations including the right to do business and the obligation to pay taxes. Sometimes one hears of a law referring to "natural persons." That is to differentiate them from corporations which are persons, but not natural persons.

Business corporations were invented hundreds of years ago to promote risky ventures such as voyages to explore the new world. Prior to the use of corporations, if the venture failed, persons engaged in business faced the possibility of unlimited liability. By using a corporation, many people were able to invest fixed sum of money for a new venture, and if the venture made money, they shared the profits. If the venture failed, the most they could lose was their initial investment.

The reasons for having a corporation are the same today: Corporations allow investors to put up money for new ventures without risk of further liability. While our legal system is making people liable in more and more situations, the corporation remains one of the few shields from liability which has not yet been abandoned.

Before forming a corporation you should be familiar with these common corporate terms which will be used in the text:

Shareholder is a person who owns stock in a corporation. In most small corporations the shareholders are the same as the officers and directors, but in large corporations most shareholders are not officers or directors. Sometimes small corporations have shareholders who are not officers, such as when the stock is in one spouse's name and the other spouse runs the business. Specific laws regarding issuance of shares and shareholders' rights vary from state to state and are listed in the various state statutes.

Officers usually include a president, secretary, treasurer and vice president. These persons typically run the day-to-day affairs of the business. They are elected each year by the Board of Directors. In most states, one person can hold all of the offices of a corporation. (See Appendix A.)

Board of Directors is the controlling body of a corporation which makes major corporate decisions and elects the officers. It usually meets just once a year. In most states a corporation can have one director (who can also hold all offices and own all the stock.) In a small corporation, the board members are usually also officers.

Registered Agent/Resident Agent (hereinafter referred to as Registered Agent) is the person designated by the corporation to receive legal papers which may be served on the corporation. The registered agent should be regularly available at the **registered office** of the corporation. The registered office can be the corporate office, the office of the corporation's attorney or other person who is the registered agent.

A person accepting the position as registered agent must often sign a statement that he or she understands the duties and responsibilities of the position. These are spelled out in the state statutes listed in Appendix A.

The **Articles of Incorporation/Certificate of Incorporation** (hereinafter referred to as Articles of Incorporation) is the document which is filed with the appropriate state agency to start the corporation. [In all but 12 states, this agency is the Secretary of State. In these other states it may be called the Department of State, the Division of Corporations, or some similar name. Appendix A will tell you what name is used in your state. For simplicity, the phrase "Secretary of State" will be used to designate this agency.] In most cases it legally needs to contain only five basic statements. Some corporations have lengthy Articles of Incorporation, but this just makes it harder to make changes in the corporate structure. It is usually better to keep the Articles short and put the details in the Bylaws. (See Appendix B for form Articles of Incorporation.)

Bylaws are the rules governing the structure and operation of the corporation. Typically the bylaws will set out rules for the Board of Directors, Officers, Shareholders and will explain corporate formalities.

Chapter 2
Should You Incorporate?

Before forming a corporation, a business owner or prospective business owner should become familiar with the advantages and disadvantages of incorporating.

A. **Advantages.** The following are some of the advantages that a corporation has over other forms of businesses such as sole proprietorships and partnerships.

    1. **Limited Liability.** The main reason for forming a corporation is to limit the liability of the owners. In a sole proprietorship or partnership the owners are personally liable for the debts and liabilities of the business and creditors can even go after all of their personal assets to collect business debts. If a corporation is formed and operated properly, the owners can be protected from all such liability.

        Examples: a. If several people are in *partnership* and one of them makes many extravagant purchases in the name of the partnership, the other partners can be held liable for the full amount of all such purchases. The creditors can take the bank accounts, cars, real estate and other property of any partner to pay the debts of the partnership. If only one partner has money, he may have to pay all of the debts run up by all the other partners. When doing business in the *corporate form*, the corporation may go bankrupt and the shareholders may lose their initial investment, but the creditors cannot touch the personal assets of the owners.

b.   If a person owns a taxi business and one of the drivers causes a terrible accident, the owner can be held liable for the full amount of the damages. If the taxi driver was on drugs and killed several people and the damages amount to millions of dollars more than the insurance coverage, the owner may lose everything he has. On the other hand if the business is formed as a corporation only the corporation would be liable and if there was not enough money, the stockholder(s) still couldn't be touched personally. An example which carried this to the extreme is as follows: there was once a business owner who had hundreds of taxis. He put one or two in each of hundreds of different corporations which he owned. Each corporation only had minimum insurance and when one taxi was involved in an accident, the owner only lost the assets of that corporation.

But Note: If a corporate officer or shareholder does something negligent himself, or signs a debt personally, or guarantees a corporate debt, the corporation will not protect him from the consequences of his own act or from the debt. Also, if a corporation does not follow the proper corporate formalities, it may be ignored by a court and the owner may be held personally liable. The formalities include having separate bank accounts, holding meetings, and keeping minutes. When a court ignores a corporate structure and holds the owners liable, it is called **piercing the corporate veil**.

2.   **Continuous Existence.** In all states (except Mississippi) a corporation may have a perpetual existence. When a sole proprietor or partner dies, the assets may go to their heirs but the business does not exist any longer. If the surviving spouse or other heirs of a business owner want to continue the business in their own names they will be considered a new business even if they are using the assets of the old business. With a partnership the death of one partner may cause a dissolution of the business.

Examples: a.   If a person dies owning a sole proprietorship, his or her spouse may want to continue the business. That person may inherit all of the assets but will have to start a new business. This means getting new licenses and tax numbers, registering the name and establishing credit from scratch. With a corporation, the business continues with all of the same licenses, bank accounts, etc.

b. If one partner dies, a partnership may be forced out of business. The surviving heirs can force the sale of their share of the assets of the partnership even if the surviving partner needs them to continue the business. If he does not have the money to buy the heirs out, the business may have to be dissolved. With a corporation, the heirs would only inherit stock. With properly drawn documents, the business could continue.

3. **Ease of Transferability.** A corporation and all of its assets and accounts may be transferred by the simple assignment of a stock certificate. With a sole proprietorship or partnership, each of the individual assets must be transferred and the accounts, licenses and permits must be individually transferred.

Example: If a sole proprietorship is sold, the new owner will have to get a new license (if one is required), set up his own bank account and apply for a new taxpayer identification number. The title to any vehicles and real estate will have to be put in his name and all open accounts will have to be changed to his name. He will probably have to submit new credit applications. With a corporation, all of these items remain in the same corporate name. **Note:** In some cases the new owners will have to submit personal applications for such things as credit or liquor licenses.

4. **Ownership Can Be Transferred Without Control.** By distributing stock, the owner of a business can share the profits of a business without giving up control.

Example: If an individual wants to give his children some of the profits of his business, he can give them stock and pay dividends to them without giving any management control. This would not be possible with a partnership or sole proprietorship.

5. **Ease of Raising Capital.** A corporation may raise capital by selling stock or borrowing money. A corporation does not pay taxes on money it raises by the sale of stock.

Example: If a corporation wants to expand, the owners can sell off 10%, 25% or 45% of the stock and still remain in control of the business. Many individuals considering investing may be more willing to invest if they know they will have a piece of the action.

Note: There are strict rules about the sale of stock with criminal penalties and triple damages for violators.

6.   **Separate Record Keeping.** A corporation is required to keep its bank accounts and records separate from the accounts of its stockholders, whereas a sole proprietor or partnership may mix business and personal accounts, a practice which often causes confusion in record keeping and is not recommended.

7.   **Tax Advantages.** There are several tax advantages which are available only to corporations.

Examples: a.   Medical insurance for families may be fully deductible.

b.   A tax deferred trust can be set up for a retirement plan.

c.   Losses are fully deductible for a corporation whereas an individual must prove there was a profit motive before deducting losses.

8.   **Ease of Estate Planning.** Shares of a company can be distributed more easily with a corporation than with a partnership. Heirs can be given different percentages and control can be limited to the appropriate parties.

9.   **Prestige.** The name of a corporation often sounds more prestigious than the name of a sole proprietor. John Smith d/b/a Acme Builders sounds like a lone man. Acme Builders, Incorporated, sounds like it might be a large operation. It has been suggested that an individual who is president of a corporation looks more successful than one doing business in their own name. The appearance of a business starts with its name.

10.   **Separate Credit Rating.** A corporation has its own credit rating which may be better or worse than the shareholder's personal credit rating. A corporate business can go bankrupt and the shareholder's personal credit will remain unharmed. Conversely, the shareholder's credit may be bad but the corporation will maintain a good rating.

B.　　　　**Disadvantages**

1.　　　**Extra Tax Return and Annual Report.** A corporation is required to file its own tax return. This is a bit longer and more complicated than the form required for a sole proprietorship or partnership. Additional expenses for the services of an accountant may be required. Typically, a corporation must also file a simple annual report with the state (which lists names and addresses of officers and directors) and pay a fee.

2.　　　**Separate Records.** The shareholders of a corporation must be careful to keep their personal business separate from the business of the corporation. The corporation must have its own records, keep minutes of meetings, and keep all corporate money separate from personal money.

3.　　　**Extra Expenses.** There are additional expenses in operating a corporation. People who employ an attorney to form their corporation pay a lot more than people who use this book. Also, in some states a shareholder may have to pay unemployment or worker's compensation insurance covering himself which he wouldn't have to pay as a sole proprietor.

4.　　　**Checking Accounts.** Typically, checks made out to a corporation cannot be cashed by a shareholder. They must be deposited into a corporate account. Some banks have higher fees just for businesses which are incorporated.

Chapter 3
Which Type of Corporation is Best?

A. **In-state Corporation or Foreign Corporation.** A person wishing to form a corporation must decide whether the corporation will be an in-state corporation or a "foreign" corporation. A **foreign corporation** is one incorporated in a state other than the one in which it will do business. In the past there was some advantage to incorporating in Delaware, since that state had very liberal laws regarding corporations, and many national corporations are incorporated there. There are books on the market which advise readers to incorporate in Delaware. Some suggest Nevada. However, in most cases there are no additional advantages to incorporating in another state.

If you form a corporation in a state other than your own, you will probably be required to have an agent or an office in that state and then you will have to register as a foreign corporation doing business in your state. This is more expensive and more complicated than incorporating in your own state. Also, if you are sued by someone who is not in your state, they can sue you in the state in which you are incorporated. This would probably be more expensive for you than a suit filed in your local court.

B. **S-Corporation or C-Corporation.** A corporation has a choice of how it wants to be taxed. It can make the election at the beginning of its existence or at the beginning of a new tax year. The choices are as follows:

1. **S-Corporation.** Formerly called a "Subchapter S corporation," this type of corporation pays no income tax and may only be used for small businesses. All of the income or losses of the corporation for the year are

passed through to the shareholders who report them on their individual returns. At the end of each year the corporation files an "information return" listing all of its income, expenses, depreciation, etc., and sends each shareholder a notice of his share as determined by percentage of stock ownership.

a. **Advantages.** Using this method avoids double taxation and allows the pass-through of losses and depreciation. For tax purposes, the business is treated as a partnership. Since many businesses have tax losses during the initial years due to start-up costs, many businesses elect S status and switch over to C-Corporation status in later years. Be aware that once a corporation terminates its S status there is a five year waiting period before it can switch back. Typically, S-Corporations do not have to pay state corporate income tax.

b. **Disadvantages.** If stockholders are in high income brackets their share of the profits will be taxed at those rates. Shareholders who do not "materially participate" in the business cannot deduct losses. Some fringe benefits such as health and life insurance may not be tax deductible.

c. **Requirements.** To qualify for S-Corporation status the corporation must:

  • have no more than 35 shareholders, none of whom are non-resident aliens or corporations, all of whom consent to the election, (shares owned by a husband and wife jointly are considered owned by one shareholder),

  • have only one class of stock,

  • not be a member of an "affiliated group,"

  • generate at least 20% of its income in this country and have no more than 20% of its income from "passive" sources (interest, rents, dividends, royalties, securities transactions), and

  • file Form 2553 with the IRS before the end of the 15th day of the third month of the tax year for which it is to be effective and have it approved.

2. **C-Corporation.** A C-Corporation pays taxes on its net earnings at corporate rates. Salaries of officers, directors and employees are taxable to them and deductible to the corporation. However, money paid out in dividends is taxed twice. It is taxed at the corporation's rate as part of its

profit and then at the individual stockholders' rates as income when distrubuted by the corporation to them.

a. **Advantages.** If taxpayers are in a higher tax bracket than the corporation and the money will be left in the company for expansion, taxes are saved. Fringe benefits such as health, accident and life insurance are deductible expenses.

b. **Disadvantages.** Double taxation of dividends by the federal government. Also, most states have an income tax which only applies to C-Corporations and applies to all income over a certain amount. **Note:** Neither of these taxes applies to money taken out as salaries, and many small business owners take all profits out as salaries to avoid double taxation and state income tax. But there are rules requiring that salaries be reasonable. If a stockholder's salary is deemed to be too high relative to his job, the salary may be considered to be partially a dividend and subject to double taxation.

c. **Requirements.** None. All corporations are C-Corporations unless they specifically elect to become S-Corporations.

3. **Closely Held Corporation Election.** A closely held corporation election is beneficial for many small businesses. It's purpose is to place restrictions on the transferability of stock. Often it obligates a shareholder to offer to the corporation or the shareholders the opportunity to purchase the stock before offering it to any outside purchaser. If the corporation and shareholders reject the offer, they typically must still consent to who the transferee (buyer) of the shares will be.

C. **Inc. or P.A./P.C.** Under the laws of most states, certain types of services can only be rendered by a corporation if it is a "professional association" ("P.A."), or "professional service corporation" ("P.C."). These include such professionals as attorneys, physicians, certified public accountants, veterinarians, architects, life insurance agents, and chiropractors. For simplicity these will be referred to as professional service corporations. A professional service corporation typically has specific rules under the state incorporation statutes.

1. **Purpose.** A professional service corporation must usually have one specific purpose spelled out in the articles of incorporation and that purpose must be to practice a specific profession. It may not engage in any other business, but it may invest its funds in real estate, stocks, bonds, mortgages or other types of investments. A professional service corporation may change its purpose to another legal purpose, but it will then no longer be a professional service corporation.

2. **Name.** In most states, the name of a professional service corporation must contain the word "chartered," "professional association," or "professional corporation," or the abbreviation "P.A." or "P.C." Typically, it may not use the words "company," "corporation" or "incorporated" or any abbreviation of these.

3. **Shareholders.** According to the law in most states, only persons licensed to practice a profession may be shareholders of a professional service corporation engaged in that practice. A shareholder who loses the right to practice must immediately sever all employment with, and financial interests in, such a corporation. If such a shareholder does not, the corporation may be dissolved by the state. No shareholder may enter into a voting trust or other similar arrangement with anyone.

4. **Merger.** A professional service corporation may not merge with any other corporation except a professional service corporation which is licensed to perform the same type of service.

5. **Requirements.** Most states have very specific requirements for the formation of professional service corporations. They often require specific language in the articles, charter or bylaws. For this type of corporation you should consult an attorney or obtain a copy of your state statute on professional corporations.

D. **Not-for-profit corporations.** Not-for-profit corporations are usually used for social clubs and churches and are beyond the scope of this book. While they are similar to for-profit corporations in many aspects, such as limited liability and the required formalities, there are additional state and federal requirements which must be met. For information on books dealing with not-for-profit corporations, contact the publisher.

Chapter 4
Start-up Procedures

A.   **Name Check.** The first thing to do before starting a corporation is to thoroughly check out the name you wish to use to be sure it is not already being used by someone else. Many businesses have been forced to stop using their name after spending thousands of dollars promoting it.

      1.   **Local Records.** To check the name you wish to use, call the corporate records office of the Secretary of State's office (see Appendix A.) In some states, to check for unincorporated businesses using the name, you should check the records office in the local county courthouse. If you will have offices in several counties it is best to check the records in each county. Because some businesses neglect to register their name, it is also advisable to check local phone books.

      2.   **National Records.** Occasionally local businesses will get letters from national companies ordering them to stop using a name which has been registered as a federal trademark. To be sure this will not happen you can have a search done of the records in the trademark office in Washington D.C.. If you plan to do business out of state it is especially important to search such records. Some public libraries have computer access to the records of the trademark office and can perform a search for a nominal fee. Another place to check is the *Trade Names Directory* which is available at many libraries. A more thorough search would include other directories and phone books of major cities. Some companies offer to perform searches of the trademark office and other directories and phone books. The cost is typically $100 to $200. One such company is:

Government Liaison Services, Inc.
P. O. Box 10648
Arlington, VA 22209
(703) 524-8200

3. **Name Reservation.** It is possible to reserve a name for a corporation for a certain period and fee (see Appendix A.) However, this is usually pointless because it is usually just as easy to file the articles as it is to reserve the name. One possible reason for reserving a name would be to hold it while waiting for a trademark name search to arrive.

4. **Similar Names.** Sometimes it seems like every good name is taken. But a name can often be modified slightly or used on a different type of product or service. If there is a "TriCounty Painting, Inc." in Cleveland it may be possible to use something like "TriCounty Painting of Cincinnati, Inc.," if you are in a different part of the state. Try different variations if your favorite is taken. Another possibility is to give the corporation one name and then do business under a fictitious name. (See subsection 7. which follows.)

    Example: If you want to use the name "Flowers by Freida" in Miami and there is already a "Flowers by Freida, Inc." in Orlando, you might incorporate under the name "Freida Jones, Inc." and then register the corporation as doing business under the fictitious name "Flowers by Freida." Unless "Flowers by Freida, Inc." has registered a trademark for the name either in Florida or nationally, you will probably be able to use the name. **Note:** You should realize that you might run into complications later, especially if you decide to expand into other areas of the state or other states. One protection available would be to register the name as a trademark. This would give you exclusive use of the name anywhere that it was not already being used. (See subsection 6. which follows.)

5. **Forbidden Names.** A corporation may not use certain words in its name if there would be a likelihood of confusion. There are state and federal laws which control the use of these words. In most cases your application will be rejected if you use a forbidden word. Some of the words which may not be used in some states without special licenses or registration are:

Assurance	Disney
Bank	Insurance
Banker	Olympic
Banking	Trust
Credit Union	

6. **Trademarks.** The name of a business may not be registered as a trademark, but the name of goods or services may be registered and such registration will grant the holder exclusive rights to use that name except in areas where someone else has used the name. A trademark may be registered either in your state or in the entire country.

    Each trademark is registered for a certain "class" of goods. Thus you may usually register the name "Zapata" chewing gum even if someone has registered the name "Zapata" for use on shoes. One exception to this rule is if the name is so well known that your use would cause confusion. For example, you could not use "Coca-Cola" as a brand of shoes because people are so familiar with the Coca-Cola company that they might think the company started a line of shoes. If you want to register the mark for several types of goods or services you must register it for each different class into which the goods or services fall, and pay a separate fee for each category.

    For protection within each state, the mark may be registered with the department of state. The cost varies from state to state and application forms and instructions can be obtained through the same department.

    For protection across the entire United States, the mark can be registered with the United States Patent and Trademark Office and the fee is about $200. The procedure for federal registration is more complicated than state registration and is explained in the book *How to Register a United States Trademark* available from Sphinx Publishing (Tel 800-226-5291) for $14.95.

7. **Fictitious Names.** A corporation may operate under a fictitious or assumed name just as an individual can. This is done when a corporation wants to operate several businesses under different names or if the business name is not available as a corporate name. Fictitious names are either registered in each county or are registered statewide with the secretary of state. However, registering a fictitious name does not give the registrant any rights to the name. While corporate names are carefully checked by the Secretary of State and disallowed if they are similar to others, fictitious names are filed without checking and any number of people may register the same name. The cost of registering a fictitious name varies. Application forms and instructions can be obtained from your local courthouse or Secretary of State.

    Note: When a fictitious name is used by a corporation, the corporate name should also be used. This is because if the public does not see that they are dealing with a corporation, they may be able to "pierce the corporate veil" and sue the stockholders individually.

B. **Articles of Incorporation.** To create a corporation a document must be filed with the Secretary of State. In most states this document is called the Articles of Incorporation; however, in some states it may be called the "Certificate of Incorporation," Articles of Association, or the "Charter." This document is referred to as the Articles of Incorporation throughout this book. Some corporations have long, elaborate articles which spell out numerous powers and functions, but most of this is unnecessary. The powers of corporations are spelled out in state law and do not have to be repeated. Attorneys can charge a lot more for articles of incorporation which are long and look complicated. The main reason to keep the articles of incorporation short is to avoid having to amend them later.

1. **Requirements.** Typically, state law requires only a minimum amount of detail be included in the Articles of Incorporation. Some things, such as the purpose of the corporation, regulations for the operation of the corporation, and a par value of the stock may be spelled out in the articles of incorporation. This is not advisable unless required since any changes would necessitate the complicated process of amending the articles. It is better to spell these terms out in the bylaws. The matters typically required to be contained in the articles and a few of the optional provisions are:

a. **Name of the corporation.** Many states require that the corporation name contain one of the following six words:
- Incorporated
- Inc.
- Corporation
- Corp.
- Company
- Co.

(The specific name requirements for your state are listed in Appendix A.)

The reason for the requirement is so that persons dealing with the business will be on notice that it is a corporation. This is important in protecting the shareholders from liability.

b. **Address of the corporation.** The street address of the principal office and the mailing address of the corporation must be provided.

c. **The number of shares of stock the corporation is authorized to issue.** This is usually an even number such as 100, 1000 or 1,000,000.

In some cases it may be advantageous to issue different classes of stock such as common and preferred or voting and non-voting but such matters should be discussed with an attorney or accountant.

If there are different classes of stock, then the articles of incorporation must contain a designation of the classes and a statement of the preferences, limitations and relative rights of each class. In addition, if there are to be any preferred or special shares issued in series, then the articles must explain the relative rights and preferences and any authority of the board of directors to establish preferences. Any preemptive rights must also be spelled out.

This book will explain how to form a corporation with one class of stock. It is usually advisable to authorize double or quadruple the amount of stock which will be initially issued. The unissued stock can be issued later if more capital is contributed by a shareholder or by a new member of the business.

One important point to keep in mind when issuing stock is that the full par value must be paid for the shares. If this is not done then the shareholder can later be held liable for the full par value. For more important information about issuing stock see Chapter V.

d. **The name of the registered agent and the address of the registered office along with the agent's acceptance.** Each corporation must have a registered agent and a registered office. The registered office can be the business office of the corporation if the registered agent works out of that office, it can be the office of another individual who is the registered agent (such as an attorney) or it may be a corporate registered agent's office. Technically it may not be a residence unless that address is also a business office of the corporation. Penalty for failure to comply can be the inability to maintain a lawsuit and a possible fine.

e. **The name and address of the incorporator of the corporation.** This may be any person, even if that person has no future interest in the corporation. There have been companies in state capitols which will, on a moment's notice, have someone run over to the Secretary of State to file corporate articles which are later assigned to the real parties in interest. However, in some states those who maintain deposits of funds with the Secretary of State are allowed to file articles by facsimile, so there is less running these days.

f. **Duration.** The duration of the corporation need not be mentioned if it is to be perpetual. If not, the duration must be specified in the articles.

g. **Effective date.** A specific effective date may be in the articles but is not required. Articles are effective upon filing. If an effective date is specified, state law varies as to the time before or after the filing in which the Articles of Incorporation are effective.

2.   **Execution.** The Articles of Incorporation must be signed by the incorporator and dated. Typically, the registered agent must sign a statement accepting his duties as such. This is sometimes done as a separate form or sometimes on the same form as the articles.

3.   **Forms.** Articles of Incorporation need not be on any certain form. They can be typed on blank paper or can be on a fill-in-the-blank form. In the back of this book are forms of Articles of Incorporation for each state. (Appendix B.)

4.   **Filing.** The Articles of Incorporation must be filed with the Secretary of State by sending them to the address listed in Appendix A along with the filing fees. The fees (as of 1993) are listed in Appendix A as well. If you wish to receive a certified copy of the articles, the cost is additional. In many states this is an unnecessary expense since a certified copy is rarely, if ever, needed. Ask your bank if a certified copy will be required by it. Usually the better alternative is to enclose a photocopy along with the articles and ask that it be "stamped with the filing date" and returned. See Appendix C for a letter to the Secretary of State.

In most states the return time for the articles is usually a week or two. If there is a need to have them back quickly you might be able to send them and have them returned by a courier such as Federal Express with prepaid return. Call your secretary of state for details.

C.   **Shareholder Agreement.** When there are two or more shareholders in a corporation they should consider drawing up a shareholder agreement. This document spells out what is to happen in the event of a disagreement between the parties. In closely held corporations the minority shareholders have a risk of being locked into a long term enterprise with little or no way to withdraw their capital. A shareholder agreement is a fairly complicated document and should be drawn up by an attorney. This may be costly but the expense should be weighed against the costs of lengthy litigation should the parties break up. Some of the things which may be addressed in such an agreement are as follows:

Veto by minority shareholder
Greater than majority voting requirement
Cumulative voting
Deadlocks
Arbitration
Dissolution
Compulsory buy-out
Preemptive rights
Restrictions on transfers of shares
Refusal of a party to participate

D.   **Organizational Paperwork.** Every corporation must have bylaws and must maintain a set of minutes of its meetings. The bylaws must be adopted at the first meeting and the first minutes of the corporation will record the proceedings of the organizational meeting.

1.   **Bylaws.** The bylaws are the rules for organization and operation of the corporation. They are required by state law. Appendix C contains one form of bylaws for a simple corporation. To complete it, fill in the name and state of the corporation, the city of the main office of the corporation, the proposed date of the annual meeting (this can be varied each year as needed), and the number of directors to be on the board.

2.   **Waiver of Notice.** Before any meeting of the incorporators, board of directors or shareholders can be held, formal notice must be given to the parties of the meeting. Since small corporations often need to have meetings on short notice and do not want to be bothered with formal notices, it is customary to have all parties sign written waivers of notice. Waivers of notice are included in the book for the organizational meeting and for the annual and special meetings (Appendix C).

3.   **Minutes.** As part of the formal requirements of operating a corporation, minutes must be kept of the meetings of shareholders and the board of directors. Usually only one meeting of each is required each year unless there is some special need for a meeting in the interim (such as the resignation of an officer). The first minutes will be the minutes of the organizational meeting of the corporation. At this meeting the officers and directors are elected, the bylaws, corporate seal and stock certificates are adopted and other organizational decisions made. Most of the forms are self-explanatory. (Appendix C).

4.   **Resolutions.** When the board of directors or shareholders make major decisions it is usually done in the form of a resolution. At the organizational meeting some important resolutions which may be passed are choosing a bank and adopting S-corporation status (Appendix C).

E.   **Tax Forms.**

1.   **Form SS-4 (Employer Identification Number).** Prior to opening a bank account, the corporation must obtain a "Taxpayer Identification Number" which is the corporate equivalent of a social security number. This is done by filing Form SS-4 which is included in this book (Appendix C). This usually takes two or three weeks, so it should be filed early. Send the form to your local Internal Revenue Service Center.

If you need the identification number quickly you may be able to obtain it by calling the IRS. Be sure to have your SS-4 form complete before calling and have it in front of you.

When you apply for this number you will probably be put on the mailing list for other corporate tax forms. If you do not receive these you should call your local IRS office and request the forms for new businesses. These include Circular E explaining the taxes due, the W-4 forms for each employee, the tax deposit coupons and the Form 941 quarterly return for withholding.

2.　**Form 2553 (S-Corporation).** If your corporation is to be taxed as an S-corporation, you must file Form 2553 with the IRS within 75 days of incorporation. As a practical matter you should sign and file this at your incorporation meeting, otherwise you may forget. This form is included in this book (Appendix C).

3.　**State Tax Forms.** In most states there is a state corporate income tax. In some states you will be exempt from corporate income tax if you are an S-Corporation, but you will need to file a form to let them know that you are exempt.

If you will be selling or renting goods or services at retail, you may be required to collect state sales and use taxes. To do this you will need to register and in most cases pay a registration fee. In some states and in some businesses you will be required to post a bond covering the taxes you will be collecting. There may be other taxes which your state requires. Contact your state taxing authority and ask for the forms available for new corporations.

F.　**Corporate Supplies.**

1.　**Corporate Kits.** A corporation needs to keep a permanent record of its legal affairs. This includes the original charter, minutes of all meetings, records of the stock issued, transferred and cancelled, fictitious names registered, and any other legal matters. The records are usually kept in a ring binder. Any ring binder will do, but it is possible to purchase a specially prepared "corporate kit" which has the name of the corporation printed on it and usually contains forms such as minutes and stock certificates. Most of these items are included with this book, so purchasing such a kit is unnecessary unless you want to have a fancy leather binder or specially printed stock certificates.

Some sources for corporate kits are:

Ace Industries, Inc.
54 NW 11th St.
Miami, FL 33136-9978
(305) 358-2571
(800) 433-2571

Midstate Legal Supply Co., Inc.
P. O. Box 2122
Orlando, FL 32802
(407) 299-8220   (800) 327-9220

Corpex
1440 5th Ave.
Bayshore, NY 11106
(800) 221-8181

2.   **Corporate Seal.** One thing that is not included with this book is a corporate seal. This must be specially made for each corporation. Most corporations use a metal seal like a notary's seal to emboss the paper. This can be ordered from an office supply company. In recent years many have been using rubber stamps for corporate seals. These are cheaper, lighter and easier to read. Rubber stamp seals can also be ordered from office supply stores, printers and specialized rubber stamp companies. The corporate seal should contain the full, exact name of the corporation, the word "SEAL" and the year of incorporation. It may be round or rectangular.

3.   **Stock Certificates and Offers to Purchase Stock.** Some corporations are no longer required to issue stock certificates to represent shares of ownership. However, as a practical matter it is a good idea to do so. This shows some formality and gives each person tangible evidence of ownership. If you do issue shares, the face of each certificate must show the corporate name, the state law under which the corporation was organized, the name of the shareholder(s), and the number, class and series of the stock. The certificate must be signed by one or more officers designated by the bylaws or the board of directors.

If there are two or more classes or series of stock, the front or back of the certificate must disclose that, upon request and without charge, the corporation will provide to the shareholder the preferences, limitations and relative rights of each class or series, the preferences of any preferred stock, and the board of directors' authority to determine rights for any subsequent classes or series. If there are any restrictions, they must be stated on the certificate or a statement must be included that they are available without charge.

The stock certificates can be fancy, with engraved eagles, or they can be typed or even handwritten. If you purchase a "corporate kit" then you will receive certificates printed with your company's name on them. A stock certificate which may be photocopied is included in this book.

Before any stock is issued the purchaser should submit an "Offer to Purchase Stock" (Appendix C). The offer states that it is made pursuant to IRS Code §1244. This section originally allowed greater tax deductions in case the stock became worthless. With the new tax laws no longer differentiating between long- and short-term capital gains, this would not make a difference, but if the laws again change it may become important. Some thought should be given to the way in which the ownership of the stock will be held. Stock owned in one person's name alone is subject to probate upon death. Making two persons joint owners of the stock (joint tenants with full rights of survivorship) would avoid probate upon the death of one of them. However, taking a joint owner's name off in the event of a disagreement (such as divorce) could be troublesome. Where a couple jointly operates a business, joint ownership would be best. But where one person is the sole party involved in the business the desire to avoid probate should be weighed against the risk of losing half the business in a divorce.

4. **Taxes.** Some states levy a tax on the issue or transfer of stock. The amount and means of calculating the tax varies from state to state. Check with the Secretary of State, or your county government tax office to find out if any such tax is charged, how to calculate the amount of tax, and how to go about paying it.

G. **Organizational Meeting.** The real birth of the corporation takes place at the initial meeting of the incorporators and the initial board of directors. At this meeting the stock is issued and the officers and board of directors are elected. Other business may also take place, such as opting for S-Corporation status or adopting employee benefit plans.

Usually, minutes, stock certificates and tax and other forms are prepared before the organizational meeting and used as a script for the meeting. They are then signed at the end of the meeting.

Those items in the following agenda designated with an asterisk (*) are forms found in Appendix C of this book. These forms may be photocopied and used, or modified as necessary to fit your situation.

The agenda for the initial meeting is usually as follows:
1. Signing the Waiver of Notice of the Meeting (Appendix C)
2. Noting Persons Present
3. Presentation and Acceptance of Articles of Incorporation (the copy returned by the Secretary of State)
4. Election of Directors
5. Adoption of Bylaws (Appendix C)
6. Election of Officers
7. Presentation and Acceptance of Corporate Seal
8. Presentation and Acceptance of Stock Certificates (Appendix C)
9. Designation of Bank (Appendix C)
10. Resolution Accepting Stock Offers (Appendix C) (Use Form H, Bill of Sale, if property is traded for stock.)

11. Resolution to Pay Expenses
12. Adoption of Special Resolutions such as S-Corp. Status
(Appendix C)
13. Adjournment

The stock certificates are usually issued at the end of the meeting, but in some cases, such as when a prospective shareholder does not yet have money to pay for them, they are issued when paid for.

To issue the stock, the certificates at the end of this book should be completed by adding the name of the corporation, a statement that the corporation is organized under the laws of the state of incorporation, the number of shares the certificate represents and the person to whom the certificate is issued. Each certificate should be numbered in order to keep track of it. A record of the stock issuance should be made on the stock transfer ledger and on the "stubs." (Appendix C) The stubs should be cut apart on the dotted lines, punched and inserted in the ring binder. Some states may charge taxes or fees upon the issuance of stock. You should check with your Secretary of State's office to determine all necessary taxes or fees. (See Appendix A).

H. **Minute Book.** After the organizational meeting you should set up your minute book. As noted previously this can be a fancy leather book or a simple ring binder. The minute book usually contains the following:

1. Title page ("Corporate Records of _____")
2. Table of contents
3. The letter from the Secretary of State acknowledging receipt and filing of the Articles of Incorporation
4. Copy of the Articles of Incorporation
5. Copy of any fictitious name registration
6. Copy of any trademark registration
7. Waiver of Notice of Organizational Meeting
8. Minutes of Organizational Meeting
9. Bylaws
10. Sample stock certificate
11. Offer to purchase stock
12. Tax forms:
   a. Form SS-4 and Employer Identification Number
   b. Form 2553 and acceptance
   c. Any State form necessary along with State tax number
13. Stock ledger
14. Stock stubs

I. **Bank Account.** A corporation will need a bank account. Typically, checks payable to a corporation cannot be cashed by a shareholder; they must be deposited into an account.

1.   **Fees.** Unfortunately many banks charge ridiculous rates to corporations for the right to put their money in the bank. You can tell how much extra a corporation is being charged when you compare a corporate account with a personal account with similar activity.

Usually there is a complicated scheme of fees with charges for each transaction. Some banks are even bold enough to charge companies for making a deposit! (Twenty-five cents for the deposit plus 10¢ for each check which is deposited. Deposit 30 checks and this will cost you $3.25!) Often the customer is granted an interest credit on the balance in the account, but this is usually small and if the credit is larger than the charges, you lose the excess.

Fortunately, some banks have set up reasonable fees for small corporations. Some charge no fees if a balance of $1000 or $2000 is maintained. Because the fees can easily amount to hundreds of dollars a year, it pays to shop around. Even if the bank is relatively far from the business, using bank-by-mail can make the distance meaningless. But don't be surprised if a bank with low fees raises them. The author knows of one company which had to change banks four times in one year as each one raised its fees or was bought out by a bank with higher fees.

As the banking industry gets deeper into trouble, less and less banks are offering reasonable fees for corporate checking accounts. But you can usually find loopholes if you use your imagination. One trick is to open a checking account and a money market account. (Money market accounts typically pay higher interest and do not charge for making deposits. You can only write about three checks a month but you can usually make unlimited deposits.) Then make all of your deposits into the money market account and just pay bills out of the checking account, transferring funds as needed.

Another way to save money in bank charges is to order checks from a private source rather than through the bank. These are usually much cheaper than those the bank offers. If the bank officer doesn't like the idea when you are opening the account, just wait until your first batch of bank checks runs out and switch over at that time.

2.   **Paperwork.** All you should need to open a corporate bank account is a copy of your Articles of Incorporation and your federal tax identification number and perhaps a business license. Some banks, however, want more and they sometimes don't even know what they want. After opening numerous corporate accounts with only those items, one individual recently encountered a bank employee who wanted "something certified so we know who your officers are. Your attorney will know what to draw up." He explained that he was an attorney and was the president,

secretary and treasurer of the corporation and would write out and sign and seal whatever they wanted. The bank employee insisted that it had to be a nice certificate signed by the secretary of the corporation and sealed. So a statement was typed out in legalese, a gold foil seal was put on it and the bank opened the account. If you have trouble opening the account you can use the "Banking Resolution" included with this book (Appendix C), or you can make up a similar form.

J.   **Licenses.** In some states, counties and municipalities are authorized to levy a license fee or tax on the "privilege" of doing business. (Some would argue that earning a living is a basic human right and not a privilege, but this is not a philosophy book.) Before opening your business you need to find out if any such license is required. Businesses which perform work in several cities, such as builders, may need to obtain a license from each city or county in which they persorm work or have an office.

Every state also has laws requiring the licensing of certain types of businesses or professions. Some states regulate more types than others. Just because you didn't need a license in one state is no guarantee that you won't need one if you move to a new state.

Be sure to find out if zoning allows your type of business before buying or leasing property. Usually the licensing departments will check the zoning before issuing your license.

Chapter 5
Selling Corporate Stock

A.   **Securities Laws.** Every issuance of securities is subject to both federal and state securities laws. Securities means stock in the company (common and preferred) and debt (notes, bonds, etc.). The law is so broad that any instrument which represents an investment in an enterprise, where the investor is relying on the efforts of others, is considered a security. Even a promissory note has been held to be a security. Once an investment is determined to involve a security, strict rules apply. There can be criminal penalties, and civil damages can also be awarded to purchasers, if the rules are not followed. The rules are designed to protect people who put up money as an investment in a business. In the stock market crash in the early 1930s many people lost their life savings in swindles and the government wants to be sure that it won't happen again. Unfortunately, the laws can also make it difficult to raise capital for many honest businesses. Even a small corporation can raise capital by seeking investors. The investors can pay capital to the corporation in exchange for stock. This sale of corporate stock is a sale of securities subject to the securities laws.

The basic requirement when selling securities is that investors be given full disclosure of the risks involved in an investment. To accomplish this the law usually requires that the securities must either be registered with the federal Securities and Exchange Commission and/or a similar state regulatory body, and that lengthy disclosure statements be compiled and distributed. The sale must be exempt from registration.

The law is complicated and strict, and the penalties so harsh that most lawyers won't handle securities matters. You will not be able to get through the registration process on your own. But, like your decision to incorporate without a lawyer, you may wish to consider some alternatives when attempting to raise capital without a lawyer:

1. Borrow the money as a personal loan from the friends or relatives. The disadvantage is that you will have to pay them back personally if the business fails. However, you may have to do that anyway if they are close relatives or if you don't follow the securities laws.

2. Tailor your stock issuance to fall within the exemptions in the securities laws. There are some exemptions for small businesses in the securities laws that may apply to your transaction. (The anti-fraud provisions always apply, even if the transaction is exempt from registration.) Some exemptions are explained below, but you should make at least one appointment with a securities lawyer to be sure you have covered everything and that there have not been any changes in the law. Often you can pay for an hour or so of a securities lawyer's time for $100 or $150 and just ask questions about your plans. He or she can tell you what not to do and what your options are. Then you can make an informed decision.

B. **Exemptions From Securities Laws.** In most situations where one person, a husband and wife or a few partners run a business, and all parties are active in the enterprise, securities laws do not apply to their issuance of stock to themselves. These are the simple corporations which are the subject of this book. As a practical matter, if your father or aunt wants to put up some money for some stock in your business you probably won't get in trouble. They probably won't seek triple damages and criminal penalties if your business fails. (This can't be said of your father-in-law in the event he becomes your ex-father-in-law some day!)

There are other special situations which may also be exempt. The following is a brief summary of exemptions available in some states.

1. **The Typical State Law Private Placement Exemption.** This can apply if all of the following are true:

    •There are 35 or fewer purchasers of shares

    •No commissions are paid to anyone to promote the stock

    •No advertising or general solicitation is used to promote the stock

    •All material information (including financial information) regarding the stock issuance and the company is given to or accessible to all shareholders

    •A three day right of recision is given.

These rules may sound simple on the surface but there are many more rules, regulations and court cases explaining each one in more detail. For example, what does "35 persons" mean? Sounds simple, but it can mean more than 35 persons. Spouses, persons whose net worth exceeds a million dollars, and founders of the corporation may not be counted in some circumstances. Each state has its own "blue sky" requirements and exemptions. If you are going to raise money from investors, check with a qualified securities lawyer.

2. **Federal Private Offering Exemption.** This can apply if:

> •All persons to whom offers are made are financially astute, are participants in the business or have a substantial net worth,

> •No advertising or general solicitation is used to promote the stock,

> •The number of persons to whom the offers are made is limited,

> •The shares are purchased for investment and not for immediate resale,

> •The persons to whom the stock is offered are given all relevant information (including financial information) regarding the issuance and the corporation. Again, there are numerous court cases explaining each aspect of these rules, including such questions as what is a "financially astute" person, and

> • A filing claiming the exemption is made upon the United States Securities and Exchange Commission.

3. **Federal Intrastate Offering Exemption.** You may be exempt from federal registration if you offer shares only to bona fide residents of one state.

It is important to note that in all cases where exemption from securities laws is sought there can be no general advertising or solicitation and all persons to whom the stock is offered must be given full information about the offering and the condition of the corporation. (In some cases, to be safe, promoters list everything they can think of which is negative about themselves and the stock.) This is a very serious aspect of forming a corporation and is one time when you should consider seeking assistance from a qualified lawyer.

C. **Payment for Shares.** When issuing stock it is important that full payment be made by the purchasers. If the shares have a par value and the payment is in cash, then the cash must not be less than the par value. In most states promissory notes cannot be used in payment for shares. The shares must not be issued until the payment has been received by the corporation.

1. **Trading Property for Shares.** In many cases organizers of a corporation have property they want to contribute for use in starting up the business. This is often the case where an on-going business is incorporated. To avoid future problems the property should be traded at a fair value for the shares. The directors should pass a resolution stating that they agree with the value of the property. When the stock certificate is issued in exchange for the property, a bill of sale should be executed by the owner of the property detailing everything which is being exchanged for the stock.

2. **Taxable Transactions.** In cases where property is exchanged for something of value, such as stock, there is often income tax due as if there had been a sale of the property. Fortunately, §351 of the IRS Code allows tax-free exchange of property for stock if the persons receiving the stock for the property or for cash *end up owning* at least 80% of the voting and other stock in the corporation. If more than 20% of the stock is issued in exchange for services instead of property and cash, then the transfers of property will be taxable and treated as a sale for cash.

3. **Trading Services for Shares.** In some cases the founders of a corporation wish to issue stock to one or more persons in exchange for their services to the corporation. It has always been possible to issue shares for services which have previously been performed. Some states make it unlawful to issue shares for promises to perform services in the future.

Chapter 6
Running a Corporation

A. **Day to Day Activities.** There are not many differences between running a corporation and any other type of business. The most important point to remember is to keep the corporation's affairs separate from personal affairs. The corporation should not be continually making loans to its shareholders and funds of the corporation and individual shareholders should not be commingled.

Another important point to remember is to always refer to the corporation as a corporation. *Always* use the complete corporate name including designations such as "Inc." or "Corp." on *everything*. *Always* sign corporate documents with your corporate title. If you don't, you may lose your protection from liability. There have been many cases where persons forgot to put the word "pres." or "president" after their name when entering into contracts for the corporation. As a result, the persons were determined to be personally liable for performance of the contract.

B. **Corporate Records**

1. **Minute Book.** A corporation must keep minutes of the proceedings of its shareholders, board of directors, and committees of directors. The minutes should be in writing. Some states allow minutes to be kept in forms other than writing provided they can be converted into written form within a reasonable time. This would mean that they could be kept in a computer or possibly on a videotape. However, it is always best to

keep a duplicate copy or at least one written copy. Accidents can easily erase magnetic media.

2. **Record of Shareholders.** The corporation must also keep a record of its shareholders including the names and addresses and the number, class and series of shares owned. This can be kept at the registered office, principal place of business or office of its stock transfer agent (if any). A transfer ledger may be found in Appendix C.

3. **Examination of Records.** Any shareholder of a corporation has the right to examine and copy the corporation's books and records after giving proper notice before the date on which he wishes to inspect and copy. The shareholder must have a good faith reason to inspect. He must describe his purpose and the records he wishes to inspect, and state how the purpose is related to the records.

The shareholder may have his attorney or agent examine the records and may receive photocopies of the records. The corporation may charge a reasonable fee for making photocopies. If the records are not in written form, the corporation must convert them to written form. Customarily, the corporation must bear the cost of converting all of the following to written form: the articles of incorporation and any amendments, bylaws and any amendments, resolutions by the board of directors creating different rights in the stock, minutes of all shareholders' meetings and records of any action taken by the shareholders without a meeting for the past three years, written communications to all shareholders generally or of any class, names and addresses of all officers and directors, and the most recent report filed with the state corporate office. The shareholder must pay for converting any other records to writing.

If the corporation refuses to allow a shareholder to examine the records, most states allow the shareholder to seek an order from the appropriate state court. In such a case the corporation would normally have to pay the shareholder's costs and attorney fees.

4. **Balance sheets.** Most states require a corporation to furnish its shareholders with financial statements including an end of the year balance sheet and yearly income and cash flow statements, unless exempted by shareholder resolution.

C. **Annual Meetings.** Each year the corporation must hold annual meetings of the shareholders and directors. These meetings may be formal and held in a restaurant or they may be informal and held in the bedroom. A sole officer and director can hold them in his mind without verbally reciting all of the motions or taking a formal vote. The important thing is that the meetings are held and that minutes are kept, even by that one-man corporation. Regular minutes and meetings are evidence that the corporation is legitimate if the issue ever comes up in court. Minute forms for the annual meetings are included with this book. You can use them as master copies to photocopy each year. All that needs to be changed is the date, unless you actually change officers or directors or need to take some other corporate action.

D.   **Annual Report.** Most states require that each year every corporation must file an annual report. Many states make this a bi-annual requirement. Fortunately, this is a simple, often one-page, form which is sent to the corporation by the Secretary of State and may merely need to be signed. It contains such information as the federal tax identification number, officers' and directors' names and addresses, the registered agent's name and the address of the registered office. It must be signed and returned with the required fee by the date specified by the state. If it is not, then the corporation is dissolved after notice is given. Many states allow some corporate information (such as the registered office and agent) to be changed at this time without additional fees to the corporation. The corporation should be aware of this fact in order to avoid incurring needless expenses.

Chapter 7
Amending Corporate Information.

A. **Articles of Incorporation.** The Articles of Incorporation included in this book are very basic. They would have to be amended to change the name or to change the number of shares of stock. If the amendment is made before any shares are issued it may be done by the incorporator or directors by filing an amendment to the articles, referred to as Articles of Amendment,Certificate of Amendment, or some similar title. This will be referred to as Articles of Amendment in this book. These are signed by the incorporators or director stating the name of the corporation, the amendment and date adopted and a statement that it is made before any shares were issued. If the amendment is made after shares have been issued, then the Articles of Amendment must be signed by the appropriate officers. The Articles of Amendment must contain the name of the corporation, the amendments, and the date of adoption by the shareholders. If the change affects the outstanding shares, then a statement must be included describing how the change will be effected. The Articles of Amendment must be filed with the Secretary of State along with the appropriate filing fee. The fee for increasing the number of shares that the corporation is authorized to issue is more costly in many states than other amendments. The procedure for amending corporate articles depends upon who is doing the amending and at what point in time the amendment is adopted. For more information you should refer to your Secretary of State's office or your state's corporation laws.

B. **Bylaws.** The shareholders may always amend the bylaws. The board of directors may amend the bylaws unless the articles of incorporation state otherwise or unless the shareholders provide that the bylaws may not be amended by the board.

The articles of incorporation may allow a bylaw which requires a greater quorum or voting requirement for shareholders but such a requirement may not be adopted, amended or repealed by the board of directors.

A bylaw which fixes a greater quorum or voting requirement for the board of directors, and which was adopted by the shareholders may be amended or repealed only by the shareholders. If it was adopted by the board it may be amended or repealed only by the board.

C.   **Registered Agent or Registered Office.** To change the registered agent or registered office a form must be sent to the Secretary of State along with the appropriate fee. Most states provide a form for such a change. The form can be used to change both the registered agent and the registered office, or to just change one of them. If you are just changing one, such as the agent, then list the registered office as both the old address and the new address.

Chapter 8
Checklist for Forming a Simple Corporation

√ Decide on corporate name

√ Prepare and file Articles of Incorporation

√ Send for Federal Employer Identification Number (IRS Form SS-4)

√ Prepare Shareholders' Agreement, if necessary

√ Meet with accountant to discuss capitalization and tax planning

√ If necessary meet with securities lawyer regarding stock sales

√ Obtain corporate seal and ring binder for minutes

√ Pay any applicable taxes for sale or issuance of stock

√ Hold organizational meeting:
    √ Complete Bylaws, Waiver, Minutes, Offers to Purchase Stock
    √ Sign all documents and place in minute book

√ Issue stock certificates:
  √ Be sure consideration is paid
  √ Complete Bill of Sale if property is traded for stock

√ File fictitious name if one will be used

√ Get licenses

√ Open bank account

√ For S–Corporation status file form 2553

Appendix A
State-by-State Incorporation Laws

The following pages contain a listing of each state's corporation laws and fees. Because the laws are constantly being changed by state legislatures, you should call before filing your papers to confirm the fees and other requirements. The phone numbers are provided for each state.

ALABAMA

Title 10-2A, Alabama Statutes
   Secretary of State
   Corporation Division
   State Office Building, Room 536
   P.O. Box 5616
   Montgomery, AL 36130-5616
   (205) 242-5324

I. ARTICLES OF INCORPORATION

A. Must provide the office of the probate judge in the county where the initial registered office of the corporation will be located with the original and two exact copies of the Articles.

II. THE CORPORATE NAME

A. Name must contain the word "corporation", "incorporated" or abbreviation of the same.

B. Prior to incorporation, a corporate name may be reserved for a period of 120 days. Name may be reserved by telephone, subject to further secretary of state requirements.

C. There is no fee charged when initially registering the corporate name. The fee is included with the filing fee to the State of Alabama. If the name is reserved prior to filing the articles, there is no charge initially assessed. However, if the articles are not filed within 120 days, the incorporator is billed the $10.00.

III. DIRECTORS

A. Directors need not be residents of the state or shareholders of the corporation.

B. The articles or bylaws may prescribe additional requirements or qualifications.

C. A corporation must have one director or more as initially stated in articles and thereafter as many directors as stated in bylaws.

D. Director(s) are normally elected at the annual meeting of shareholders.

IV. OFFICERS

A. A corporation must have a president and secretary. Other officers may be elected or appointed in accordance with provisions set forth in the bylaws.

B. The same person may hold more than one office unless provided for otherwise in the bylaws.

C. An officer performs duties stated in the bylaws or by the board of directors or another officer to the extent consistent with the bylaws.

V. REGISTERED AGENT

A. A corporation must register an agent with the state who has an office within the state.

VI. FILING FEES

A. Articles of Incorporation
1. State of Alabama	$50.00
2. County Probate Judge	$35.00

B. Application for Name Reservation $10.00

C. Amending Articles of Incorporation
1. County Probate Judge	$10.00
2. State of Alabama	$20.00

D. Filing Annual Report State of Alabama
(minimum fee based on $5000 of capital stock) $70.00

E. Cost for Certified Copy of Any Document
        $1.00/page plus $5.00 to certify the document

Note: The minimum filing fee to initially incorporate is $85.00 for the filing of the articles and the application for name reservation. Many banks request a certified copy of the Articles prior to setting up a corporate account. Therefore, the certification cost is often necessary as well.

ALASKA

Title 10, Alaska Statutes
   Department of Commerce and Economic Development
   Division of B.S.C.
   Attention: Corporation Section
   P.O. Box 110808
   Juneau, AK 99811-0808
   (907) 465-2530

I. ARTICLES OF INCORPORATION

A. Must provide state corporation office with the original and one exact copy of the Articles.

II. THE CORPORATE NAME

A. Name must contain the word "corporation", "incorporated", "company", "limited" or abbreviation of the same.

B. Prior to incorporation, a corporate name may be reserved for a period of 120 days.

III. DIRECTORS

A. Directors need not be residents of the state or shareholders of the corporation.

B. The articles or bylaws may prescribe additional requirements or qualifications.

C. A corporation must have one director or more as initially stated in articles and thereafter as many directors as stated in bylaws.

D. Director(s) are normally elected at the annual meeting of shareholders.

IV. OFFICERS

A. A corporation must have a president, secretary and treasurer. Other officers may be elected or appointed in accordance with provisions set forth in the bylaws.

B. The same person may hold as many as two offices, except for the president and secretary. If all issued stock is owned by one person, he may hold all offices.

C. An officer performs duties stated in the bylaws or by the board of directors or another officer to the extent consistent with the bylaws.

V. REGISTERED AGENT

A. A corporation must register an agent with the state who has an office within the state.

VI. FILING FEES

A. Articles of Incorporation	$250.00
B. Change of Registered Agent & Acceptance	$15.00
C. Application for Name Reservation	$15.00
D. Amending Articles of Incorporation	$15.00
E. Filing Biennial Report	$100.00
F. Cost for Certified Copy of Articles	$10.00

Note: The filing fees include $150.00 for the actual filing of the articles and $100.00 for the initial biennial report.

ARIZONA

Title 10, Arizona Statutes
    Arizona Corporation Commission
    P.O. Box 6019
    Phoenix, AZ 85005
    (602) 542-3135

I.   ARTICLES OF INCORPORATION
    A.   Two persons must act as incorporators.
    B.   Must provide state corporation office with the original and one exact copy of the Articles. The copy will be returned to the incorporators and within 60 days. It must be published for 3 consecutive publications in a newspaper of general circulation in the county of the known place of business.

II.   THE CORPORATE NAME
    A.   Name must contain the word "corporation", "incorporated", "company", "limited" or abbreviation of the same.
    B.   Prior to incorporation, a corporate name may be reserved for a period of 120 days.

III.   DIRECTORS
    A.   Directors need not be residents of the state or shareholders of the corporation.
    B.   The articles or bylaws may prescribe additional requirements or qualifications.
    C.   A corporation must have one director or more as initially stated in articles and thereafter as many directors as stated in bylaws.
    D.   Director(s) are normally elected at the annual meeting of shareholders.

IV.   OFFICERS
    A.   A corporation must have a president, one or more vice presidents, a secretary and a treasurer. Other officers may be elected or appointed in accordance with provisions set forth in the bylaws.
    B.   The same person may hold more than one office except for the president and the secretary.
    C.   An officer performs duties stated in the bylaws or by the board of directors or another officer to the extent consistent with the bylaws.

V.   REGISTERED AGENT
    A.   Corporation must have a statutory agent at a known place of business within the state.

VI.   FILING FEES
    A. Articles of Incorporation $60.00
    B. Amending Articles of Incorporation $25.00
    C. Filing Annual Report $45.00
    D. Cost for Certified Copy of Any Document $5.00 + .50/page
    E. Fee for Publishing Articles or Amendments in County of Business
            Variable, depending on the newspaper and length of articles

ARKANSAS

Title 4, Chapter 27, Arkansas Statutes
    Secretary of State
    Corporation Division
    State Capital, Room 58
    Little Rock, AR 72201
    (501) 682-5151

I.   ARTICLES OF INCORPORATION
    A.   Must be printed or typewritten in English.
    B.   Must provide state corporation office with duplicate originals of the Articles.

II.   THE CORPORATE NAME
    A.   Name must indicate its corporate character. This can be done by using such words as "corporation", "incorporated", "company", "limited" or abbreviation of the same.
    B.   Prior to incorporation, a corporate name may be reserved for a period of 120 days.

III.   DIRECTORS
    A.   Directors need not be residents of the state or shareholders of the corporation.
    B.   The articles or bylaws may prescribe additional requirements or qualifications.
    C.   A corporation must have one director or more as initially stated in articles and thereafter as many directors as stated in bylaws. The number of directors may be increased or decreased by amending the articles or bylaws in a manner set forth in the articles or bylaws.
    D.   Director(s) are normally elected at the annual meeting of shareholders.

IV.   OFFICERS
    A.   A corporation must have two officers. Other officers may be elected or appointed in accordance with provisions set forth in the bylaws.
    B.   The same person may hold more than one office.
    C.   An officer performs duties stated in the bylaws or by the board of directors or another officer to the extent consistent with the bylaws.
    D.   One officer shall be responsible for preparing the records of any director or shareholder meeting.

V.   REGISTERED AGENT
    A.   A corporation must register an agent with the state who has an office within the state.

VI.   FILING FEES
    A. Articles of Incorporation $50.00
    B. Change of Registered Agent' Name/Address $25.00
    C. Application for Name Reservation $25.00
    D. Amending Articles of Incorporation $50.00
    E. Filing Annual Report (Minimum) $50.00
    F. Cost for Certified Copy of Any Document $5.00 + .50/page

Note: Corporation must have a minimum of $300.00 paid for shares of stock prior to commencing business. In filing the annual report, fee is based on franchise tax assessed.

CALIFORNIA

California Corporation Code, Title 1
    Secretary of State
    Corporate Division
    Attn: Legal Review
    1230 J Street
    Sacramento, CA 95814
    (916) 445-0620

I. ARTICLES OF INCORPORATION

A. Must provide state corporation office with the original copy of the Articles.

II. THE CORPORATE NAME

A. Name must not contain words which are likely to mislead the public or contain the words "bank", "trust", "trustee" or related words.

B. Prior to incorporation, a corporate name may be reserved for a nonrenewable period of 60 days.

III. DIRECTORS

A. Directors need not be residents of the state or shareholders of the corporation.

B. The articles or bylaws may prescribe additional requirements or qualifications.

C. A corporation must have three directors or more as initially stated in articles and thereafter as many directors as stated in bylaws. However, when there are less than three shareholders, there need be only a corresponding number of directors.

D. Director(s) are normally elected at the annual meeting of shareholders.

IV. OFFICERS

A. A corporation must have a president and/or a chairman of the board, a secretary and a chief financial officer. Other officers may be elected or appointed in accordance with provisions set forth in the bylaws.

B. The same person may hold more than one office unless provided for otherwise in the bylaws.

C. An officer performs duties stated in the bylaws or by the board of directors or another officer to the extent consistent with the bylaws.

V. REGISTERED AGENT

A. A corporation must register an agent with the state who has an office within the state.

VI. FILING FEES

A. Articles of Incorporation	$100.00
B. Change of Registered Agent & Acceptance	$5.00
C. Application for Name Reservation	$10.00
D. Amending Articles of Incorporation	$30.00
E. Filing Annual Report	$5.00
F. Cost for Certified Copy of Any Document	$5.00
G. Minimum annual franchise tax	*$800.00

* Must be paid when Articles are filed, for a total of $900.00 to incorporate.

COLORADO

Title 7, Colorado Revised Statutes
    Secretary of State
    Corporations Office
    1560 Broadway, Suite 200
    Denver, CO 80202
    (303) 894-2251

I. ARTICLES OF INCORPORATION

A. Must provide state corporation office with two sets of original Articles.

B. Must record certificate of incorporation in each county where the corporation owns real property.

II. THE CORPORATE NAME

A. Name must contain the word "corporation", "incorporated", "company" or "limited" or abbreviation of the same.

B. Prior to incorporation, a corporate name may be reserved for a period of 120 days and is renewable for another 120 days. Name may not be reserved by telephone, although a name search can be done by this method.

III. DIRECTORS

A. Director(s) must be at least 18 years of age but need not be a resident of the state or a shareholder of the corporation.

B. The articles or bylaws may prescribe additional requirements or qualifications.

C. A corporation must have three directors or more as initially stated in articles and thereafter as many directors as stated in bylaws. However, when there are less than three shareholders, there need be only a corresponding number of directors.

D. Director(s) are normally elected at the annual meeting of shareholders.

IV. OFFICERS

A. A corporation must have a president, secretary and treasurer who are elected by the board and must be at least 18 years of age. Other officers may be elected or appointed in accordance with provisions set forth in the bylaws.

B. The same person may hold more than one office except the offices of president and secretary and unless prohibited from doing so in the bylaws.

C. An officer performs duties stated in the bylaws or by the board of directors to the extent consistent with the bylaws.

V. REGISTERED AGENT

A. A corporation must register an agent with the state who has an office within the state.

VI. FILING FEES

A. Articles of Incorporation	$50.00
B. Change of Registered Agent & Acceptance	$10.00
C. Application for Name Reservation	$10.00
D. Amending Articles of Incorporation	$25.00
E. Filing Annual Report	$25.00
F. Cost for Certified Copy of Any Document	
	$1.00 + $1.00 per page

CONNECTICUT

Title 33, Connecticut Statutes
  Secretary of State
  30 Trinity Street
  Hartford, CT 06106
  (203) 566-4128

I. CERTIFICATE OF INCORPORATION
  A. Must be printed or typewritten in English.
  B. Must provide state corporation office with the original and one exact copy of the Certificate.

II. THE CORPORATE NAME
  A. Name must contain the word "corporation", "incorporated", "company", "limited", "Society per Azion" or abbreviation of the same.
  B. Prior to incorporation, a corporate name may be reserved for a period of 120 days.

III. DIRECTORS
  A. Directors need not be residents of the state or shareholders of the corporation.
  B. The certificate or bylaws may prescribe additional requirements or qualifications.
  C. A corporation must have three directors or more as initially stated in articles and thereafter as many directors as stated in bylaws. However, when there are less than three shareholders, there need be only a corresponding number of directors.
  D. Director(s) are normally elected at the annual meeting of shareholders.

IV. OFFICERS
  A. A corporation must have a president and secretary. Other officers may be elected or appointed in accordance with provisions set forth in the bylaws.
  B. The same person may hold more than one office except for the offices of president and secretary.
  C. An officer performs duties stated in the bylaws or by the board of directors to the extent consistent with the bylaws.

V. REGISTERED AGENT
  A. Corporation must register with the state an agent at an office within the state.

VI. FILING FEES
A. Certificate of Incorporation	$50.00
B. Change of Registered Agent & Acceptance	$25.00
C. Application for Name Reservation	$30.00
D. Amending Certificate of Incorporation	$50.00
E. Filing Biennial Report	$125.00
F. Cost for Certified Copy of Any Document	$25.00
G. Organizational Tax (up to 20,000 shares)	$150.00

Note: The minimum fee for initial incorporation is $325.00 for the filing fee, organizational tax and initial biennial report.

DELAWARE

Title 8, Delaware Code
  Secretary of State
  Division of Corporations
  John G. Townsend Building
  Duke of York Street
  Dover, DE 19901
  (302) 739-3073

I. CERTIFICATE OF INCORPORATION
  A. Must be printed or typewritten in English.
  B. Must provide state corporation office with the original and one exact copy of the Certificate.
  C. Must record a copy of the Certificate in the county where the registered office is located.

II. THE CORPORATE NAME
  A. Name must contain the word "corporation", "incorporated", "association", "company", "club", "foundation", "fund", "institute", "society", "union", "syndicate" or "limited" or abbreviation of the same.
  B. Prior to incorporation, a corporate name may be reserved for a period of 30 days. Name may be reserved by telephone by calling (900) 555-2677.

III. DIRECTORS
  A. Directors need not be residents of the state or shareholders of the corporation.
  B. The articles or bylaws may prescribe additional requirements or qualifications.
  C. A corporation must have one director or more as initially stated in articles and thereafter as many directors as stated in bylaws.
  D. Director(s) are normally elected at the annual meeting of shareholders.

IV. OFFICERS
  A. A corporation may have officers which are elected or appointed in accordance with provisions set forth in the bylaws or determined by the directors.
  B. The same person may hold more than one office unless provided for otherwise in the bylaws.
  C. An officer performs duties stated in the bylaws or by the board of directors or another officer to the extent consistent with the bylaws.
  D. One officer shall be responsible for preparing the records of any director or shareholder meeting.

V. REGISTERED AGENT
  A. A corporation must register an agent with the state who has an office within the state.

VI. FILING FEES
A. Receiving & Indexing Certificate of Incorporation	$50.00
B. Application for Name Reservation	$10.00
C. Amending Articles of Incorporation	$100.00
(includes filing fee, receiving & indexing)	
D. Filing Annual Report	$20.00
E. Cost for Certified Copy of Any Document	
	$20.00 + $1.00 per page
F. Incorporation Tax (for up to 1500 shares)	$15.00

Note: The minimum filing fee to initially incorporate is $50.00 for the receiving and indexing of the Certificate of Incorporation, the Incorporation Tax and one Certified Copy.

DISTRICT OF COLUMBIA

Title 29, District of Columbia Code

    Department of Consumer and Regulatory Affairs
    Corporation Division
    614 H. Street NW, Room 407
    Washington, D.C. 20001
    (202) 727-7283

I. ARTICLES OF INCORPORATION

    A. Must be printed or typewritten in English.

    B. Must provide Department of Consumer and Regulatory Affairs with duplicate originals.

II. THE CORPORATE NAME

    A. Name must contain the word "corporation", "incorporated", "company", or "limited" or abbreviation of the same.

    B. Prior to incorporation, a corporate name may be reserved for a period of 60 days.

III. DIRECTORS

    A. Directors need not be a shareholder of the corporation.

    B. The articles or bylaws may prescribe additional requirements or qualifications.

    C. A corporation must have three directors or more as initially stated in articles and thereafter as many directors as stated in bylaws.

    D. Director(s) are normally elected at the annual meeting of shareholders.

IV. OFFICERS

    A. A corporation must have a president, one or more vice presidents, secretary and treasurer. Other officers may be elected or appointed in accordance with provisions set forth in the bylaws.

    B. The same person may hold more than one office except of president and secretary unless prohibited from doing so in the bylaws.

    C. An officer performs duties stated in the bylaws or by the board of directors or another officer to the extent consistent with the bylaws.

V. REGISTERED AGENT

    A. A corporation must register an agent with the state who has an office within the state.

VI. FILING FEES

A. Articles of Incorporation	$42.00
B. Designation of Registered Agent & Acceptance	$3.00
C. Application for Name Reservation	$7.00
D. Amending Articles of Incorporation*	$22.00
E. Filing Annual Report	$100.00
F. Cost for Certified Copy of Any Document	$5.00

* Except for changes in numbers of shares

FLORIDA

Chapter 607, Florida Statutes

    Secretary of State
    Division of Corporations
    P.O. Box 6327
    Tallahassee, FL 32314
    (904) 488-9000

I. ARTICLES OF INCORPORATION

    A. Must be printed or typewritten in English.

    B. Must provide state corporation office with the original and one exact copy of the Articles.

II. THE CORPORATE NAME

    A. Name must contain the word "corporation", "incorporated", "company" or abbreviation of the same.

    B. Prior to incorporation, a corporate name may be reserved for a non-renewable period of 120 days.

III. DIRECTORS

    A. Director(s) must be a natural person, 18 years of age, but need not be a resident of the state or a shareholder of the corporation.

    B. The articles or bylaws may prescribe additional requirements or qualifications.

    C. A corporation must have one director or more as initially stated in articles and thereafter as many directors as stated in bylaws.

    D. Director(s) are normally elected at the annual meeting of shareholders.

IV. OFFICERS

    A. A corporation must have the officers described in its bylaws or appointed in accordance with provisions set forth in the bylaws.

    B. The same person may hold more than one office unless provided for otherwise in the bylaws.

    C. An officer performs duties stated in the bylaws or by the board of directors or another officer to the extent consistent with the bylaws.

    D. One officer shall be responsible for preparing the records of any director or shareholder meeting.

V. REGISTERED AGENT

    A. A corporation must register an agent with the state who has an office within the state.

VI. FILING FEES

A. Articles of Incorporation	$35.00
B. Designation of Registered Agent & Acceptance	$35.00
C. Application for Name Reservation	$35.00
D. Amending Articles of Incorporation	$35.00
E. Filing Annual Report	
	$200.00
F. Cost for Certified Copy of Any Document	$52.50

Note: The minimum filing fee to initially incorporate includes the filing of the Articles of Incorporation and Designation of Registered Agent.

GEORGIA

Title 22, Georgia Code
Secretary of State
2 Martin Luther King, Jr. Drive
Suite 315, West Tower
Atlanta, GA 30304
(404) 656-2817

I. ARTICLES OF INCORPORATION

A. Must be printed or typewritten in English, although name of corporation may be in another language.

B. Must provide state corporation office with the original and one exact copy of the Articles.

C. Must publish notice of intent to incorporate pursuant to Georgia law.

II. THE CORPORATE NAME

A. Name must contain the word "corporation", "incorporated", "company", "limited" or abbreviation of the same.

B. Prior to incorporation, a corporate name may be reserved for a nonrenewable period of 90 days.

III. DIRECTORS

A. Directors must be at least 18 years of age but need not be a resident of the state or a shareholder of the corporation.

B. The articles or bylaws may prescribe additional requirements or qualifications.

C. A corporation must have one director or more as initially stated in articles and thereafter as many directors as stated in bylaws.

D. Director(s) are normally elected at the annual meeting of shareholders.

IV. OFFICERS

A. A corporation must have the officers elected or appointed in accordance with provisions set forth in the bylaws.

B. The same person may hold more than one office unless provided for otherwise in the bylaws.

C. An officer performs duties stated in the bylaws or by the board of directors or another officer to the extent consistent with the bylaws.

D. One officer shall be responsible for preparing the records of any director or shareholder meeting.

V. REGISTERED AGENT

A. A corporation must register an agent with the state who has an office within the state.

VI. FILING FEES

A. Articles of Incorporation	$60.00
B. Application for Name Reservation	no fee
C. Amending Articles of Incorporation	$20.00
D. Filing Annual Report	$15.00
E. Fee for Publishing Notice of Intent to Incorporate	$40.00

Note: The fee for initially incorporating is $100.00 This includes filing the articles of incorporation and publishing the notice of intent to incorporate.

HAWAII

Title 23, Hawaii Revised Statutes
Secretary of State
Business Registration Division
Department of Commerce and Consumer Affairs
1010 Richards Street
P.O. Box 40
Honolulu, HI 96810
(808) 586-2727

I. ARTICLES OF INCORPORATION

A. Must provide state corporation office with the original Articles.

II. THE CORPORATE NAME

A. Name must contain the word "corporation", "incorporated", "limited" or abbreviation of the same.

B. Prior to incorporation, a corporate name may be reserved for a period of 120 days. Name may be reserved by written application only.

III. DIRECTORS

A. At least one member of the board of directors must be a resident of the state.

B. The articles or bylaws may prescribe additional requirements or qualifications.

C. A corporation must have three directors or more as initially stated in articles and thereafter as many directors as stated in bylaws. However, if the corporation has less than three shareholders, then only a corresponding number of directors is required.

D. Director(s) are normally elected at the annual meeting of shareholders.

IV. OFFICERS

A. A corporation must have a president, one or more vice presidents, a secretary and a treasurer. Other officers may be elected or appointed in accordance with provisions set forth in the bylaws.

B. The same person may hold more than one office, including that of president and secretary, unless provided for otherwise in the bylaws. However, if the corporation has two or more directors, it must have two or more officers.

C. An officer performs duties stated in the bylaws or by the board of directors or another officer to the extent consistent with the bylaws.

V. FILING FEES

A. Articles of Incorporation	$50.00
B. Application for Name Reservation	$10.00
C. Amending Articles of Incorporation	$25.00
D. Filing Annual Report	$15.00
E. Cost for Certified Copy of Any Document	
$10.00/document plus .25/page for copying.	

IDAHO

Title 30, Idaho Code
    Secretary of State
    Statehouse, Room 203
    Boise, ID 83720
    (208) 334-2300

I. ARTICLES OF INCORPORATION

A. Must provide state corporation office with duplicate originals.

II. THE CORPORATE NAME

A. Name must contain the word "corporation", "incorporated", "company", "limited" or abbreviation of the same.

B. Prior to incorporation, a corporate name may be reserved for a period of four months.

III. DIRECTORS

A. Directors need not be residents of the state or shareholders of the corporation.

B. The articles or bylaws may prescribe additional requirements or qualifications.

C. A corporation must have one director or more as initially stated in articles and thereafter as many directors as stated in bylaws.

D. Director(s) are normally elected at the annual meeting of shareholders.

IV. OFFICERS

A. A corporation must have a president, one or more vice presidents, a secretary and a treasurer. Other officers may be elected or appointed in accordance with provisions set forth in the bylaws.

B. The same person may hold more than one office except same person cannot hold both president and secretary positions.

C. An officer performs duties stated in the bylaws or by the board of directors or another officer to the extent consistent with the bylaws.

V. REGISTERED AGENT

A. A corporation must register an agent with the state who has an office within the state.

VI. FILING FEES

A. Articles of Incorporation	$60.00
B. Change of Registered Agent's Name/Address	no fee
C. Application for Name Reservation	$10.00
D. Amending Articles of Incorporation	$20.00
E. Filing Annual Report	no fee
F. Cost for Certified Copy of Any Document	
	$2.00/certification and .25/page

ILLINOIS

Chapter 32, Illinois Statutes
    Secretary of State
    Office of Corporations Department
    3rd Floor
    Centennial Building
    Springfield, IL 62756
    (217) 782-6875
    (217) 782-7880

I. ARTICLES OF INCORPORATION

A. Must provide state corporation office with duplicate originals of the Articles.

II. THE CORPORATE NAME

A. Name must contain the word "corporation", "incorporated", "company" or "limited" or abbreviation of the same.

B. Prior to incorporation, a corporate name may be reserved for a period of 90 days. Informal requests to check name availability will be answered by telephone.

III. DIRECTORS

A. Directors need not be residents of the state or shareholders of the corporation.

B. The articles or bylaws may prescribe additional requirements or qualifications.

C. A corporation must have one director or more as initially stated in articles and thereafter as many directors as stated in bylaws.

D. Director(s) are normally elected at the annual meeting of shareholders.

IV. OFFICERS

A. A corporation must have the officers elected or appointed in accordance with provisions set forth in the bylaws.

B. The same person may hold more than one office unless provided for otherwise in the bylaws.

C. An officer performs duties stated in the bylaws or by the board of directors or another officer to the extent consistent with the bylaws.

D. One officer shall be responsible for preparing the records of any director or shareholder meeting.

V. REGISTERED AGENT

A. A corporation must register an agent with the state who has an office within the state.

VI. FILING FEES

A. Articles of Incorporation	$100.00
B. Designation of Registered Agent & Acceptance	$5.00
C. Application for Name Reservation	$25.00
D. Amending Articles of Incorporation	$25.00
E. Filing Annual Report	$15.00 + fee based on capital

Note: The initial franchise tax is assessed at the rate of $1.50/$1,000 on the paid-in capital represented in Illinois, with a minimum tax of $25.00. Therefore, for paid-in capital up to $16,667.00, the minimum fee for initial incorporation is $100.00.

INDIANA

Title 23, Indiana Statutes
> Secretary of State
> Room 155, State House
> 302 W. Washington, Room E018
> Indianapolis, IN 46204
> (317) 232-6576 or
> (317) 232-6531

I. ARTICLES OF INCORPORATION
    A. Must be printed or typewritten in English.
    B. Must provide state corporation office with the original and one exact copy of the Articles.

II. THE CORPORATE NAME
    A. Name must contain the word "corporation", "incorporated", "company", "limited" or abbreviation of the same.
    B. Prior to incorporation, a corporate name may be reserved for a period of 120 days. Name may be reserved only by written application.

III. DIRECTORS
    A. Directors need not be residents of the state or shareholders of the corporation.
    B. The articles or bylaws may prescribe additional requirements or qualifications.
    C. A corporation must have one director or more as initially stated in articles and thereafter as many directors as stated in bylaws.
    D. Director(s) are normally elected at the annual meeting of shareholders.

IV. OFFICERS
    A. A corporation must have the officers described in its bylaws or appointed in accordance with provisions set forth in the bylaws.
    B. The same person may hold more than one office unless provided for otherwise in the bylaws.
    C. An officer performs duties stated in the bylaws or by the board of directors or another officer to the extent consistent with the bylaws.
    D. One officer shall be responsible for preparing the records of any director or shareholder meeting.

V. REGISTERED AGENT
    A. A corporation must register an agent with the state who has an office within the state.

VI. FILING FEES

A. Articles of Incorporation	$90.00
B. Change of Registered Agent's Name/Address	$30.00
C. Application for Name Reservation	$20.00
D. Amending Articles of Incorporation	$30.00
E. Filing Annual Report	$15.00
F. Cost for Certified Copy of Any Document	
	$15.00/stamp plus 1.00/page

IOWA

Chapter 490, Iowa Code
> Secretary of State
> Corporations Division
> Hoover Building
> Des Moines, IA 50319
> (515) 281-5204
> Fax: (515) 242-5953

I. ARTICLES OF INCORPORATION
    A. Must be printed or typewritten in English.
    B. Must provide state corporation office with the original and one exact copy of the Articles.

II. THE CORPORATE NAME
    A. Name must contain the word "corporation", "incorporated", "company", "limited" or abbreviation of the same.
    B. Prior to incorporation, a corporate name may be reserved for a period of 120 days. Name may be reserved only by written application.

III. DIRECTORS
    A. Directors need not be residents of the state or shareholders of the corporation.
    B. The articles or bylaws may prescribe additional requirements or qualifications.
    C. A corporation must have one director or more as initially stated in articles and thereafter as many directors as stated in bylaws.
    D. Director(s) are normally elected at the annual meeting of shareholders.

IV. OFFICERS
    A. A corporation must have the officers elected or appointed in accordance with provisions set forth in the bylaws.
    B. The same person may hold more than one office unless provided for otherwise in the bylaws.
    C. An officer performs duties stated in the bylaws or by the board of directors or another officer to the extent consistent with the bylaws.
    D. One officer shall be responsible for preparing the records of any director or shareholder meeting.

V. REGISTERED AGENT
    A. A corporation must register an agent with the state who has an office within the state.

VI. FILING FEES

A. Articles of Incorporation	$50.00
B. Change Registered Agent's Name/Address	no fee
C. Application for Name Reservation	$10.00
D. Amending Articles of Incorporation	$50.00
E. Filing Annual Report	$30.00
F. Cost for Certified Copy of Any Document	
	$5.00/certification and 1.00/page

KANSAS

Chapter 17, Kansas Statutes
    Secretary of State
    Capital Building, 2nd Floor
    300 SW 10th St.
    Topeka, KS 66612-1594
    (913) 296-2236

I. ARTICLES OF INCORPORATION

A. Must provide state corporation office with the original and a duplicate copy of the Articles.

II. THE CORPORATE NAME

A. Name must contain the word "corporation", "incorporated", "association", "church", "college", "company", "foundation", "club", "fund", "institute", "society", "syndicate", "limited", "union" or abbreviation of the same.

B. Prior to incorporation, a corporate name may be reserved for a period of 120 days.

III. DIRECTORS

A. Directors need not be residents of the state or shareholders of the corporation.

B. The articles or bylaws may prescribe additional requirements or qualifications.

C. A corporation must have one director or more as initially stated in articles and thereafter as many directors as stated in bylaws.

D. Director(s) are normally elected at the annual meeting of shareholders.

IV. OFFICERS

A. A corporation must have the officers elected or appointed in accordance with provisions set forth in the bylaws.

B. The same person may hold more than one office unless provided for otherwise in the bylaws.

C. An officer performs duties stated in the bylaws or by the board of directors to the extent consistent with the bylaws.

D. One officer shall be responsible for preparing the records of any director or shareholder meeting.

V. RESIDENT (REGISTERED) AGENT

A. Corporation must register with the state a resident agent at an office within the state.

VI. FILING FEES

A. Articles of Incorporation	$75.00
B. Application for Name Reservation	$20.00
C. Amending Articles of Incorporation (including Designation of Resident Agent)	$20.00
D. Filing Annual Report (Minimum-Maximum, depending on assets)	$20.00-2,500.00
F. Cost for Certified Copy of Any Document	
	$7.50 + .50/page if secretary supplies copy

KENTUCKY

Title 23, Kentucky Revised statutes
    Office of Secretary of State
    P.O. Box 718
    Frankfort, KY 40602-0718
    (502) 564-2848
    (502) 564-7330

I. ARTICLES OF INCORPORATION

A. Must be printed or typewritten in English.

B. Must provide state corporation office with the original and two exact copies of the Articles. After filing, one of the exact copies shall then be filed with and recorded by the county clerk of the county in which the registered office of the corporation is located.

II. THE CORPORATE NAME

A. Name must contain the word "corporation", "incorporated", "company", "limited" or abbreviation of the same.

B. Prior to incorporation, a corporate name may be reserved for a period of 120 days. A name may only be reserved in writing.

III. DIRECTORS

A. Directors need not be residents of the state or shareholders of the corporation.

B. The articles or bylaws may prescribe additional requirements or qualifications.

C. A corporation must have one director or more as initially stated in articles or bylaws and thereafter as many directors as stated in bylaws.

D. Director(s) are normally elected at the annual meeting of shareholders.

IV. OFFICERS

A. A corporation shall have the officers described in the bylaws or appointed by the board of directors in accordance with provisions set forth in the bylaws.

B. The same person may hold more than one office unless provided for otherwise in the bylaws.

C. An officer performs duties stated in the bylaws or by the board of directors or another officer to the extent consistent with the bylaws.

D. One officer shall be responsible for preparing the records of any director or shareholder meeting.

V. REGISTERED AGENT

A. A corporation must register an agent with the state who has an office within the state.

VI. FILING FEES

A. Articles of Incorporation	$40.00
B. Change Registered Agent's Name/Address	$10.00
C. Application for Name Reservation	$15.00
D. Amending Articles of Incorporation	$40.00
E. Filing Annual Report	$15.00
F. Organizational Tax (1000 shares or less)	$10.00
G. Cost for Certified Copy of Any Document	
	$5.00/certificate + .50/page

Note: The minimum filing fee to initially incorporate is $50.00 which includes filing the articles of incorporation and the organizational tax.

LOUISIANA

Title 12, Louisiana Revised Statutes
   Secretary of State
   Corporations Division
   P.O. Box 94125
   Baton Rouge, LA 70804-9125
   (504) 925-4704

I. ARTICLES OF INCORPORATION
   A. Must be printed or typewritten in English.
   B. Must provide state corporation office with the original or multiple originals of the Articles.
   C. An initial report must be filed with the Articles setting forth: 1. The name and municipal address, if any, of the corporation's registered office. 2. The full name and municipal address, if any, of each of its registered agents. 3. The names and municipal addresses, if any, of its first director(s).

II. THE CORPORATE NAME
   A. Name must contain the word "corporation", "incorporated", "limited", "company", or abbreviation of the same. If "company" or "co." are used, it may not be preceded by the word "and" or "&".
   B. Prior to incorporation, a corporate name may be reserved for a period of 60 days. Name may be reserved only by written application.

III. DIRECTORS
   A. Directors need not be residents of the state or shareholders of the corporation.
   B. The articles or bylaws may prescribe additional requirements or qualifications.
   C. A corporation must have three directors or more as initially stated in articles and thereafter as many directors as stated in bylaws. However, if there are less than three shareholders, there need only be as many directors as there are shareholders.
   D. Director(s) are normally elected at the annual meeting of shareholders.

IV. OFFICERS
   A. The board of directors of a corporation shall elect a president, secretary, treasurer and may elect one or more vice presidents. Other officers may be elected or appointed in accordance with provisions set forth in the bylaws.
   B. The same person may hold more than one office unless provided for otherwise in the articles.
   C. An officer performs duties stated in the bylaws or by the board of directors.

V. REGISTERED AGENT
   A. A corporation must register an agent with the state who has an office within the state.

VI. FILING FEES
A. Articles of Incorporation	$60.00
B. Change of Registered Agent's Name/Address	$20.00
C. Application for Name Reservation	$20.00
D. Amending Articles of Incorporation	$50.00
E. Filing Annual Report	$25.00
F. Cost for Additional Certified Copy of Any Document	$10.00

Note: The registered agent may be changed when filing the annual report without paying the $20.00 fee.

MAINE

Title 13-A Maine Revised Statutes
   Secretary of State
   Bureau of Corporations, Elections, and
   Commissions
   State House Station 101
   Augusta, ME 04333-0101
   (207) 289-3676 or
   (207) 289-3501

I. ARTICLES OF INCORPORATION
   A. Must provide state corporation office with the original and a duplicate original of the Articles.

II. THE CORPORATE NAME
   A. Name need not contain such words as "corporation", "incorporated", "company" or abbreviation of the same.
   B. Prior to incorporation, a corporate name may be reserved for a period of 120 days.

III. DIRECTORS
   A. Directors need not be residents of the state or shareholders of the corporation.
   B. The articles or bylaws may prescribe additional requirements or qualifications.
   C. A corporation must have three directors or more as initially stated in articles and thereafter as many directors as stated in bylaws. However, if the corporation has less than three shareholders, there may be an identical number of directors to shareholders.
   D. Director(s) are normally elected at the annual meeting of shareholders.

IV. OFFICERS
   A. A corporation must have a president, treasurer and clerk. Other officers may be elected or appointed by the board of directors.
   B. The same person may hold more than one office unless provided for otherwise in the bylaws.
   C. An officer performs duties stated in the bylaws or by the board of directors or another officer to the extent consistent with the bylaws.
   D. The clerk shall be responsible for preparing the records of any director or shareholder meeting.

V. REGISTERED CLERK AND OFFICE
   A. Corporation must register with the state a clerk, who is a natural person at an office within the state.

VI. FILING FEES
A. Articles of Incorporation	$75.00
B. Change of Registered Clerk & Acceptance	$20.00
C. Application for Name Reservation	$20.00
D. Amending Articles of Incorporation	$35.00
E. Filing Annual Report	$60.00
F. Cost for Certified Copy of Any Document	$5.00 + $2.00/page
G. Organization Tax (based on amount of stock-maximum of 3000 no par or $100,000 par)	$30.00

Note: The minimum filing fee to initially incorporate is $105.00 which includes the filing of the articles of incorporation and the organization tax.

MARYLAND

Corporations & Associations, Title 2, Code of Maryland
State Department of Assessments and Taxation
Corporate Charter Division
301 West Preston Street
Baltimore, MD 21201
(410) 225-1340 or
(410) 225-1330

I. ARTICLES OF INCORPORATION
A. Must provide state corporation office with the original of the Articles.

II. THE CORPORATE NAME
A. Name must contain the word "corporation", "incorporated", "company", "limited" or abbreviation of the same.

B. Prior to incorporation, a corporate name may be reserved for a period of 30 days. Name may be checked for availability by telephone at the Department of Assessments and Taxation. If several names are being checked, the request should be made in writing.

III. DIRECTORS
A. Directors need not be residents of the state or shareholders of the corporation.

B. The articles or bylaws may prescribe additional requirements or qualifications.

C. A corporation must have one director or more as initially stated in articles and thereafter as many directors as stated in bylaws.

D. Director(s) are normally elected at the annual meeting of shareholders.

IV. OFFICERS
A. A corporation must have a president, secretary and treasurer. Other officers may be elected or appointed in accordance with provisions set forth in the bylaws.

B. The same person may hold more than one office unless provided for otherwise in the bylaws. However, the same person may not serve as both president and vice president.

C. An officer performs duties stated in the bylaws or by the board of directors or another officer to the extent consistent with the bylaws.

V. RESIDENT AGENT
A. A corporation must register an agent with the state who has an office within the state.

VI. FILING FEES

A. Articles of Incorporation (not over $100,000 in capital stock)	$20.00
B. Change of Resident Agent & Acceptance	$10.00
C. Application for Name Reservation	$7.00
D. Amending Articles of Incorporation (minimum)	$20.00
E. Filing Annual Report	$100.00
F. Cost for Certified Copy of Any Document	$6.00 + $1.00/page
G. Recording Fee	$20.00

Note: The minimum filing fee to initially incorporate is $40.00, which includes the filing of the Articles of Incorporation and the Recording Fee.

MASSACHUSETTS

Chapter 156, Massachusetts General Laws
Secretary of State
Corporations Division
One Ashburton Place
17th Floor
Boston, MA 02108
(617) 727-9640 or
Citizen Information Service
(800) 392-6090

I. ARTICLES OF ORGANIZATION
A. Must provide state corporation office with the original Articles.

II. THE CORPORATE NAME
A. Name must indicate that the business is a corporation by using such words as "corporation", "incorporated" or abbreviation of the same.

B. Prior to incorporation, a corporate name may be reserved for a period of 30 days. Name availability may be checked by telephone but may be reserved only upon written request and payment of reservation fee.

III. DIRECTORS
A. Directors need not be residents of the state or shareholders of the corporation.

B. The articles or bylaws may prescribe additional requirements or qualifications.

C. A corporation must have three directors or more as initially stated in articles and thereafter as many directors as stated in bylaws. However, when there are less than three shareholders, there need be only a corresponding number of directors.

D. Director(s) are normally elected at the annual meeting of shareholders.

E. The president must also be a director unless otherwise provided in the bylaws.

IV. OFFICERS
A. A corporation must have a president, treasurer and clerk. Other officers may be elected or appointed in accordance with provisions set forth in the bylaws.

B. The same person may hold more than one office unless provided for otherwise in the bylaws.

C. An officer performs duties stated in the bylaws or by the board of directors or another officer to the extent consistent with the bylaws.

D. The clerk shall be responsible for preparing the records of any director or shareholder meeting.

V. RESIDENT (REGISTERED) AGENT
A. A corporation must register an agent with the state who has an office within the state.

VI. FILING FEES

A. Articles of Organization	$200.00
B. Change of Registered Agent's Name/Address	no fee
C. Application for Name Reservation	$15.00
D. Amending Articles of Incorporation (minimum)	$100.00
E. Filing Annual Report	$85.00
F. Cost for Certified Copy of Articles	$12.00
G. Cost for Certified Copy of Any Other Document	$7.00/first page + $2.00/additional page

MICHIGAN

Chapter 450, Michigan Compiled Laws

    Michigan Department of Commerce
    Corporation and Securities Bureau,
    Corporation Division
    P.O. Box 30054
    Lansing, MI 48909
    (517) 334-6302

I. ARTICLES OF INCORPORATION

A. Must be printed or typewritten in English.

B. Must provide state corporation office with the original and one exact copy of the Articles.

II. THE CORPORATE NAME

A. Name must contain the word "corporation", "incorporated", "company", "limited" or abbreviation of the same.

B. Prior to incorporation, a corporate name may be reserved for a period of four full calendar months. Two two-month extensions are also available. Name must be reserved by written application.

III. DIRECTORS

A. Directors need not be residents of the state or shareholders of the corporation.

B. The articles or bylaws may prescribe additional requirements or qualifications.

C. A corporation must have one director or more as initially stated in articles and thereafter as many directors as stated in bylaws.

D. Director(s) are normally elected at the annual meeting of shareholders.

IV. OFFICERS

A. A corporation must have a president, secretary, treasurer, and may have a chairman of the board, and various vice presidents. Other officers may be elected or appointed in accordance with provisions set forth in the bylaws.

B. The same person may hold more than one office unless provided for otherwise in the bylaws.

C. An officer performs duties stated in the bylaws or by the board of directors or another officer to the extent consistent with the bylaws.

V. RESIDENT AGENT

A. Corporation must register with the state a resident agent at an office within the state.

VI. FILING FEES

A. Articles of Incorporation (60,000 shares or less of stock)	$60.00
B. Change of Registered Agent & Acceptance	$5.00
C. Application for Name Reservation	$10.00
D. Amending Articles of Incorporation	$10.00
E. Filing Annual Report	$15.00

MINNESOTA

Chapter 302A Minnesota Statutes

    Secretary of State
    Division of Corporations
    180 State Office Building
    100 Constitution Ave.
    St. Paul, MN 55155
    (612) 296-2803

I. ARTICLES OF INCORPORATION

A. Must provide state corporation office with the original Articles.

II. THE CORPORATE NAME

A. Name must contain the word "corporation", "incorporated", "limited" or abbreviation of the same or the word "company" or its abbreviation, if it is not immediately preceded by "and" or "&".

B. Prior to incorporation, a corporate name may be reserved for a period of 12 months.

III. DIRECTORS

A. Directors need not be residents of the state or shareholders of the corporation.

B. The articles or bylaws may prescribe additional requirements or qualifications.

C. A corporation must have one director or more as initially stated in articles and thereafter as many directors as stated in bylaws.

D. Director(s) are normally elected at the annual meeting of shareholders or in manner prescribed in bylaws.

IV. OFFICERS

A. A corporation must have a chief executive officer and a chief financial officer, however designated. Other officers may be elected or appointed in accordance with provisions set forth in the bylaws.

B. The same person may hold more than one office unless provided for otherwise in the bylaws.

C. An officer performs duties stated in the bylaws or by the board of directors or another officer to the extent consistent with the bylaws.

V. REGISTERED AGENT

A. A corporation must register an agent with the state who has an office within the state.

VI. FILING FEES

A. Articles of Incorporation	$135.00
B. Change of Registered Agent & Acceptance	no fee
C. Application for Name Reservation	$35.00
D. Amending Articles of Incorporation	$35.00
E. Filing Annual Report	no fee if timely filed
F. Cost for Certified Copy of Articles	$8.00
with Amendments	$11.00

MISSISSIPPI

Title 79, Mississippi Code
    Secretary of State
    Business Services Division
    P.O. Box 136
    Jackson, MS 39205-0136
    (601) 359-1633

I. ARTICLES OF INCORPORATION
    A. Must be printed or typewritten in English.
    B. Must provide state corporation office with the original and one exact copy of the Articles.

II. THE CORPORATE NAME
    A. Name must contain the word "corporation", "incorporated", "company", "limited" or abbreviation of the same.
    B. Prior to incorporation, a corporate name may be reserved for a period of 180 days.

III. DIRECTORS
    A. Directors need not be residents of the state or shareholders of the corporation.
    B. The articles or bylaws may prescribe additional requirements or qualifications.
    C. The board of directors must consist of one or more individuals, initially stated in articles and with the number specified in or fixed in accordance with the articles or bylaws.
    D. Director(s) are normally elected at the annual meeting of shareholders.

IV. OFFICERS
    A. A corporation must have the officers described in its bylaws or appointed by the board of directors in accordance with provisions set forth in the bylaws.
    B. The same person may hold more than one office unless provided for otherwise in the bylaws.
    C. An officer performs duties stated in the bylaws or by the board of directors or another officer to the extent consistent with the bylaws.
    D. One officer shall be responsible for preparing the records of any director or shareholder meeting.

V. REGISTERED AGENT
    A. A corporation must register an agent with the state who has an office within the state.

VI. FILING FEES

A. Articles of Incorporation	$50.00
B. Change of Registered Agent's Name/Address	$25.00
C. Application for Name Reservation	$25.00
D. Amending Articles of Incorporation	$50.00
E. Filing Annual Report	$25.00
F. Cost for Certified Copy of Any Document	
	$10.00/certificate + 1.00/page

MISSOURI

Chapter 351, Missouri Statutes
    Secretary of State, Corporation Division
    P.O. Box 778
    Jefferson City, MO 65102
    (314) 751-2359
    (314) 751-4153

I. ARTICLES OF INCORPORATION
    A. Must be printed or typewritten in English.
    B. Must provide state corporation office with duplicate originals of the Articles.

II. THE CORPORATE NAME
    A. Name must contain the word "corporation", "incorporated", "company", "limited" or abbreviation of the same.
    B. Prior to incorporation, a corporate name may be reserved for a period of 60 days. Name availability may be checked by telephone.

III. DIRECTORS
    A. Directors need not be residents of the state or shareholders of the corporation.
    B. The articles or bylaws may prescribe additional requirements or qualifications.
    C. A corporation must have three directors or more as initially stated in articles and thereafter as many directors as stated in bylaws. However, when there are less than three shareholders, there need be only a corresponding number of directors.
    D. Director(s) are normally elected at the annual meeting of shareholders.

IV. OFFICERS
    A. A corporation must have a president and secretary. Other officers may be elected or appointed in accordance with provisions set forth in the bylaws.
    B. The same person may hold more than one office unless provided for otherwise in the bylaws.
    C. An officer performs duties stated in the bylaws or by the board of directors to the extent consistent with the bylaws.

V. REGISTERED AGENT
    A. A corporation must register an agent with the state who has an office within the state.

VI. FILING FEES
    A. Articles of Incorporation (up to 30,000 shares of stock)

	$53.00
B. Change of Registered Agent's Name/Address	$5.00
C. Application for Name Reservation	$20.00
D. Amending Articles of Incorporation	$20.00
E. Cost for Certified Copy of Any Document	$5.00 + $.50/page

MONTANA

Title 35, Montana Code
    Secretary of State
    State Capital
    Helena, MT 59620
    (406) 444-2034

I.   ARTICLES OF INCORPORATION
    A.   Must be printed or typewritten in English.
    B.   Must provide state corporation office with the original and one exact copy of the Articles.

II.   THE CORPORATE NAME
    A.   Name must contain the word "corporation", "incorporated", "company", "limited" or abbreviation of the same.
    B.   Prior to incorporation, a corporate name may be reserved for a period of 120 days.

III.   DIRECTORS
    A.   Directors need not be residents of the state or shareholders of the corporation.
    B.   The articles or bylaws may prescribe additional requirements or qualifications.
    C.   A corporation must have one director or more as initially stated in articles.
    D.   Director(s) are normally elected at the annual meeting of shareholders.

IV.   OFFICERS
    A.   A corporation must have the officers described in its bylaws or as appointed by the board of directors in accordance with the bylaws.
    B.   The same person may hold more than one office.
    C.   An officer performs duties stated in the bylaws or by the board of directors or another officer to the extent consistent with the bylaws.

V.   REGISTERED AGENT
    A.   A corporation must register an agent with the state who has an office within the state.

VI.   FILING FEES

A. Articles of Incorporation	$70.00*
B. Change of Registered Agent's Name/Address	$5.00
C. Application for Name Reservation	$10.00
D. Amending Articles of Incorporation	$15.00
E. Filing Annual Report	$10.00
F. Cost for Certified Copy of Any Document	
	$2.00 + .50 per page

*Note: At the time of incorporation, a domestic corporation must pay a license fee of a minimum of $70.00. This fee will give the corporation the authority to issue up to $50,000 worth of shares.

NEBRASKA

Chapter 21, Revised Nebraska Statutes
    Secretary of State
    Suite 1301 State Capitol
    Lincoln, NE 68509
    (402) 471-4079

I.   ARTICLES OF INCORPORATION
    A.   Must provide state corporation office with the original and one duplicate copy of the Articles. Upon return of the duplicate copy, the Articles shall be recorded in the office of the county clerk of the county where the registered office of the corporation is located.

II.   THE CORPORATE NAME
    A.   Name must contain the word "corporation", "incorporated", "company", "limited" or abbreviation of the same.
    B.   Prior to incorporation, a corporate name may be reserved for a period of 120 days.

III.   DIRECTORS
    A.   Directors need not be residents of the state or shareholders of the corporation.
    B.   The articles or bylaws may prescribe additional requirements or qualifications.
    C.   A corporation must have one director or more as initially stated in bylaws.
    D.   Director(s) are normally elected at the annual meeting of shareholders.

IV.   OFFICERS
    A.   A corporation must have a president, one or more vice presidents, a secretary and a treasurer. Other officers may be elected or appointed in accordance with provisions set forth in the bylaws.
    B.   The same person may hold more than one office.
    C.   An officer performs duties stated in the bylaws or by the board of directors to the extent consistent with the bylaws.

V.   REGISTERED AGENT
    A.   A corporation must register an agent with the state who has an office within the state.

VI.   FILING FEES

A. Articles of Incorporation (not over $10,000 of capital stock)	$40.00
B. Change of Registered Agent's Name/Address	$18.00
C. Application for Name Reservation	$15.00
D. Amending Articles of Incorporation	$15.00 + $3.00 per page
E. Cost for Certified Copy of Any Document	$10.00
F. Recording Articles of Incorporation	$15.00 + $3.00 per page

Note: The minimum filing fee to initially incorporate is $58.00 which includes the filing and recording of the Articles of Incorporation.

NEVADA

Chapter 78, Nevada Revised Statutes
   Secretary of State
   Capitol Complex
   Carson City, NV 89710
   (702) 687-5203 or
   (702) 687-5105
   Fax (702) 687-3471

I.   ARTICLES OF INCORPORATION

A.   Must provide state corporation office with the original and one exact copy of the Articles.

II.   THE CORPORATE NAME

A.   Any name which appears to be that of a natural person must contain the word "corporation", "incorporated", "company", "limited", abbreviation of the same or any other word that identifies the name as not being that of a natural person.

B.   Prior to incorporation, a corporate name may be reserved for a period of 90 days.

III.   DIRECTORS

A.   Directors need not be residents of the state or shareholders of the corporation.

B.   The articles or bylaws may prescribe additional requirements or qualifications.

C.   A corporation must have one director or more as initially stated in articles and thereafter as many directors as stated in bylaws.

D.   At least one-forth of the Directors must be elected at the annual meeting of shareholders.

IV.   OFFICERS

A.   A corporation must have a president, secretary and treasurer. Other officers may be elected or appointed in accordance with provisions set forth in the bylaws.

B.   The same person may hold more than one office unless provided for otherwise in the bylaws.

C.   An officer performs duties stated in the bylaws or by the board of directors or another officer to the extent consistent with the bylaws.

V.   REGISTERED AGENT

A.   A corporation must register an agent with the state who has an office within the state.

VI.   FILING FEES

A. Articles of Incorporation ($25,000 or less of capital stock)
                                                      $125.00
B. Change of Registered Agent's Name and Address $15.00
C. Application for Name Reservation $20.00
D. Amending Articles of Incorporation $75.00
E. Filing Annual Report
F. Cost for Certified Copy of Articles when
      a copy is provided $10.00

NEW HAMPSHIRE

Chapter 293-A, New Hampshire Revised Statutes
   Secretary of State
   State House, Room 204
   107 N. Main St.
   Concord, NH 03301
   (603) 271-3244

I.   ARTICLES OF INCORPORATION

A.   Must provide state corporation office with duplicate originals of the Articles.

II.   THE CORPORATE NAME

A.   Name must contain the word "corporation", "incorporated", "limited" or abbreviation of the same.

B.   Prior to incorporation, a corporate name may be reserved for a period of 120 days.

III.   DIRECTORS

A.   Directors need not be residents of the state or shareholders of the corporation.

B.   The articles or bylaws may prescribe additional requirements or qualifications.

C.   A corporation must have one director or more as initially stated in articles or bylaws.

D.   Director(s) are normally elected at the annual meeting of shareholders.

IV.   OFFICERS

A.   A corporation must have a president, a secretary (who shall be the registered agent) and a treasurer. Other officers may be elected or appointed in accordance with provisions set forth in the bylaws.

B.   The same person may hold more than one office unless provided for otherwise in the bylaws.

C.   An officer performs duties stated in the bylaws or by the board of directors to the extent consistent with the bylaws.

V.   REGISTERED AGENT

A.   Corporation must register with the state an agent (who is also the corporation secretary) for acceptance of service of process at an office within the state.

VI.   FILING FEES

A. Articles of Incorporation (when authorized capital stock
      exceeds $10,000 but does not exceed $15,000)   * $160.00
B. Change of Registered Agent's Name/Address $15.00
C. Application for Name Reservation $15.00
D. Amending Articles of Incorporation $35.00
E. Cost for Certified Copy of Any Document
                            $5.00 + $1.00/each additional page

*Minimum fee is $85.00 if authorized capital stock is 0-10 shares.

NEW JERSEY

Title 14A New Jersey Revised Statutes
    Secretary of State
    Division of Commercial Recording
    Trenton, NJ 08625
    (609) 530-6400

I.   CERTIFICATE OF INCORPORATION

A. Must provide state corporation office with the original and one exact copy of the Certificate.

II. THE CORPORATE NAME

A. Name must contain the word "corporation", "incorporated", "company", abbreviation of the same, or "ltd.".

B. Prior to incorporation, a corporate name may be reserved for a period of 120 days. Name must be reserved through written application.

III. DIRECTORS

A. Directors need not be residents of the state or shareholders of the corporation, but must be at least 18 years of age.

B. The certificate or bylaws may prescribe additional requirements or qualifications.

C. A corporation must have one director or more as initially stated in certificate and thereafter as many directors as stated in bylaws.

D. Director(s) are normally elected at the annual meeting of shareholders.

IV. OFFICERS

A. A corporation must have a president, secretary and treasurer. Other officers may be elected.

B. The same person may hold more than one office unless provided for otherwise in the bylaws.

C. An officer performs duties stated in the bylaws or by the board of directors to the extent consistent with the bylaws.

V. REGISTERED AGENT

A. A corporation must register an agent with the state who has an office within the state.

VI. FILING FEES

A. Certificate of Incorporation	$100.00
B. Change of Registered Agent's Name/Address	$10.00
C. Application for Name Reservation	$50.00
D. Amending Certificate of Incorporation	$50.00
E. Filing Annual Report	$20.00

NEW MEXICO

Chapter 53, New Mexico Statutes
    State Corporation Commission
    Corporation Department
    P.O. Drawer 1269
    Santa Fe, NM 87504-1269
    (505) 827-4511 or
    (505) 827-4504

I.   ARTICLES OF INCORPORATION

A. Must provide state corporation office with duplicate originals of the Articles.

II. THE CORPORATE NAME

A. Name must contain the word "corporation", "incorporated", "company", "limited" or abbreviation of the same.

B. Prior to incorporation, a corporate name may be reserved for a period of 120 days.

III. DIRECTORS

A. Directors need not be residents of the state or shareholders of the corporation.

B. The articles or bylaws may prescribe additional requirements or qualifications.

C. A corporation must have one director or more as initially stated in articles and thereafter as many directors as stated in bylaws.

D. Director(s) are normally elected at the annual meeting of shareholders.

E. Prior to serving on the board, any person appointed or elected must file an affidavit with the corporation stating he consents to serving on the board.

IV. OFFICERS

A. A corporation must have the officers described in its bylaws or appointed in accordance with provisions set forth in the bylaws.

B. The same person may hold more than one office unless provided for otherwise in the bylaws.

C. An officer performs duties stated in the bylaws or by the board of directors to the extent consistent with the bylaws.

D. One officer shall be responsible for preparing the records of any director or shareholder meeting.

V. REGISTERED AGENT

A. A corporation must register an agent with the state who has an office within the state.

VI. FILING FEES

A. Articles of Incorporation (up to $500,000.00 capital stock)	$50.00
B. Change of Registered Agent's Name/Address	$10.00
C. Application for Name Reservation	$10.00
D. Amending Articles of Incorporation	$50.00
E. Filing Annual Report	$20.00
F. Cost for Certified Copy of Any Document	$10.00 + $1.00/page

NEW YORK

Chapter 4, Consolidated Laws of New Nork
Department of State
Division of Corporations and State Records
162 Washington Avenue
Albany, N.Y. 12231-0001
(518) 473-2492 or
(518) 474-6200

I. CERTIFICATE OF INCORPORATION
A. Must be printed or typewritten in English.

B. Must provide state corporation office with the original certificate. State send certified copy to county where corporation is to be located.

II. THE CORPORATE NAME
A. Name must contain the word "corporation", "incorporated", "limited" or abbreviation of the same. The name cannot include the following words and phrases: board of trade, chamber of commerce, community renewal, state police, state trooper, tenant relocation, urban development, urban relocation, acceptance, annuity, assurance, bank, benefit, bond, casualty, doctor, endowment, fidelity, finance, guaranty, indemnity, insurance, investment, lawyer, loan, mortgage, savings, surety, title, trust, underwriter.

B. Prior to incorporation, a corporate name may be reserved for a period of 60 days. Name must be reserved through written application and can be renewed upon written request.

III. DIRECTORS
A. Directors need not be residents of the state or shareholders of the corporation, but must be at least 18 years of age.

B. The articles or bylaws may prescribe additional requirements or qualifications.

C. A corporation must have three directors or more as initially stated in articles and thereafter as many directors as stated in bylaws.

D. Director(s) are normally elected at the annual meeting of shareholders.

IV. OFFICERS
A. A corporation must have a president and secretary. Other officers may be elected or appointed in accordance with provisions set forth in the bylaws.

B. The same person may hold more than one office except the president and secretary, unless all stock is owned by that one person.

C. An officer performs duties stated in the bylaws or by the board of directors to the extent consistent with the bylaws.

D. One officer shall be responsible for preparing the records of any director or shareholder meeting.

V. REGISTERED AGENT
A. A corporation must register an agent with the state who has an office within the state.

VI. FILING FEES
A. Certificate of Incorporation $135.00
B. Certificate of Change of Registered Agent's Name/Address
$20.00
C. Application for Name Reservation $20.00
D. Amending Certificate of Incorporation $60.00
E. Cost for Certified Copy of Any Document $10.00

Note: Secretary of State must send a copy of the certificate, along with a $3.00 filing fee to the clerk of the county in which the corporation will do business. New York City's fee for this service is $25.00.

NORTH CAROLINA

Chapter 55, General Statutes of North Carolina
Corporations Division
Department of Secretary of State
300 North Salisbury Street
Raleigh, NC 27603-5909
(919) 733-4201
Office Hours: 8:00 a.m. to 5:00 p.m.
Monday through Friday

I. ARTICLES OF INCORPORATION
A. Must be printed or typewritten in English.

B. Must provide state corporation office with the original and one exact copy of the Articles.

II. THE CORPORATE NAME
A. Name must contain the word "corporation", "incorporated", "company", "limited" or abbreviation of the same.

B. Prior to incorporation, a corporate name may be reserved for a period of 120 days.

III. DIRECTORS
A. Directors need not be residents of the state or shareholders of the corporation.

B. The articles or bylaws may prescribe additional requirements or qualifications.

C. A corporation must have one director or more as initially stated in articles.

D. Director(s) are normally elected at the annual meeting of shareholders.

IV. OFFICERS
A. A corporation must have the officers as provided in accordance with provisions set forth in the bylaws.

B. The same person may hold more than one office unless provided for otherwise in the bylaws. No one person may act in more than one capacity where an action by two or more officers is required.

C. An officer performs duties stated in the bylaws or by the board of directors or another officer to the extent consistent with the bylaws.

D. One officer shall be responsible for maintaining and authenticating the records of the corporations.

V. REGISTERED AGENT
A. Corporation must register with the state agent at an office within the state.

VI. FILING FEES
A. Articles of Incorporation $100.00
B. Change of Registered Agent's Name/Address $5.00
C. Application for Name Reservation $10.00
D. Amending Articles of Incorporation $50.00
E. Filing Annual Report $10.00
F. Cost for Certified Copy of Any Document
$5.00/certification and $.50/page

NORTH DAKOTA

Title 10, North Dakota Century Code
    Secretary of State
    Capitol Building
    600 East Boulevard Avenue
    Bismarck, ND 58505-0500
    (701) 224-2900 or
    (701) 224-4289
    Fax: (701) 224-2992

I. ARTICLES OF INCORPORATION

    A. Must provide state corporation office with the original of the Articles.

II. THE CORPORATE NAME

    A. Name must contain the word "corporation", "incorporated", "company", "limited" or abbreviation of the same. If the word "company" is used, it may not be preceded by "and" or "&".

    B. Prior to incorporation, a corporate name may be reserved for a period of 12 months.

III. DIRECTORS

    A. Directors need not be residents of the state or shareholders of the corporation.

    B. The articles or bylaws may prescribe additional requirements or qualifications.

    C. A corporation must have one director or more as initially stated in articles and thereafter as many directors as stated in bylaws.

    D. Director(s) are normally elected at the annual meeting of shareholders unless there is a fixed term as prescribed in the bylaws.

IV. OFFICERS

    A. A corporation must have a president, one or more vice presidents, a secretary and a treasurer. Other officers may be elected or appointed in accordance with provisions set forth in the bylaws.

    B. The same person may hold more than one office unless provided for otherwise in the bylaws.

    C. An officer performs duties stated in the bylaws or by the board of directors to the extent consistent with the bylaws.

    D. One officer shall be responsible for preparing the records of any director or shareholder meeting.

V. REGISTERED AGENT

    A. A corporation must register an agent with the state who has an office within the state and provide the state with his social security number or federal ID number.

VI. FILING FEES

A. Articles of Incorporation	*$30.00
B. Designation of Registered Agent	$10.00
C. Capitalization Fee (first $50,000 of stock)	$50.00
D. Application for Name Reservation	$10.00
E. Amending Articles of Incorporation	$20.00
F. Filing Annual Report	$20.00
G. Cost for Certified Copy of Any Document	
	$10.00 + $1.00/4 pgs

* A minimum of $90.00 is required to incorporate. This includes the filing fee, capitization fee, and designation of registered agent.

OHIO

Title 17, Ohio Revised Statutes
    Secretary of State
    Corporations Division
    30 E. Broad St.
    State Office Tower, 14th Floor
    Columbus, OH 43266-0418
    (614) 466-3910

I. ARTICLES OF INCORPORATION

    A. Must provide state corporation office with the original and one exact copy of the Articles.

II. THE CORPORATE NAME

    A. Name must contain the word "corporation", "incorporated", "company" or abbreviation of the same.

    B. Prior to incorporation, a corporate name may be reserved for a period of 60 days. Name must be reserved through written application and payment of fee. Name availability may be checked over the telephone.

III. DIRECTORS

    A. Directors need not be residents of the state or shareholders of the corporation.

    B. The articles or bylaws may prescribe additional requirements or qualifications.

    C. A corporation must have three directors or more as initially stated in articles and thereafter as many directors as stated in bylaws. However, when there are less than three shareholders, there need be only a corresponding number of directors.

    D. Director(s) are normally elected at the annual meeting of shareholders.

IV. OFFICERS

    A. A corporation must have a president, secretary and treasurer. Other officers may be elected by the board of directors.

    B. The same person may hold more than one office unless provided for otherwise in the bylaws.

    C. An officer performs duties as determined by the board of directors.

V. RESIDENT (REGISTERED) AGENT

    A. A corporation must register an agent with the state who has an office within the state.

VI. FILING FEES

A. Articles of Incorporation (minimum fee)	$75.00
B. Change of Registered Agent's Name/Address	$3.00
C. Application for Name Reservation	$5.00
D. Amending Articles of Incorporation	$35.00
E. Cost for Certified Copy of Any Document	
	$5.00 + $1.00/page

OKLAHOMA

Title 18, Oklahoma Statutes

Secretary of State-Corporation Division
101 State Capitol Building
Oklahoma City, OK 73105
(405) 521-3911

I. CERTIFICATE OF INCORPORATION

A. Must provide state corporation office with the original and one conformed copy of the Certificate.

II. THE CORPORATE NAME

A. Name must contain the word "association", "club", "corporation", "incorporated", "company", "fund", "foundation", "institute", "society", "union", "syndicate", "limited" or abbreviation of the same.

B. Prior to incorporation, a corporate name may be reserved for a period of 60 days. Name must be reserved through written application, but informal name check may be done over the telephone.

III. DIRECTORS

A. Directors need not be residents of the state or shareholders of the corporation.

B. The certificate or bylaws may prescribe additional requirements or qualifications.

C. A corporation must have one director or more as initially stated in the bylaws unless the number of directors is fixed by the certificate.

D. Director(s) are normally elected at the annual meeting of shareholders.

IV. OFFICERS

A. A corporation must have the offices as provided for by the bylaws. The corporation must have at least two officers; a president or officer of like title and a secretary or treasurer, as stock certificates must be signed by two officers.

B. The same person may hold more than one office unless provided for otherwise in the bylaws.

C. An officer performs duties stated in the bylaws or by the board of directors to the extent consistent with the bylaws.

V. REGISTERED AGENT

A. A corporation must register an agent with the state who has an office within the state.

VI. FILING FEES

A. Certificate of Incorporation (minimum)	$50.00
B. Change of Registered Agent's Name/Address	$10.00
C. Application for Name Reservation	$5.00
D. Amending Certificate of Incorporation (minimum)	$50.00
E. Cost for Certified Copy of Any Document	
	$5.00 + $1.00/page

OREGON

Title 7, Oregon Revised Statutes

Corporation Division
State of Oregon
158 -12th St. NE
Salem, OR 97310
(503) 378-4166

I. ARTICLES OF INCORPORATION

A. Must be written in English.

B. Must provide state corporation office with the original and one exact   copy of the Articles. Articles need not be typed or printed, but must be legible.

II. THE CORPORATE NAME

A. Name must contain the word "corporation", "incorporation", "company", "limited" or abbreviation of the same.

B. Prior to incorporation, a corporate name may be reserved for a period of 120 days. Name must be reserved through written application.

III. DIRECTORS

A. Directors need not be a resident of the state or a shareholder of the corporation.

B. The articles or bylaws may prescribe additional requirements or qualifications.

C. A corporation must have one or more directors as initially stated in articles and thereafter as many directors as stated in bylaws.

D. Director(s) are normally elected at the annual meeting of shareholders.

IV. OFFICERS

A. A corporation must have a president and secretary. Other officers may be elected or appointed in accordance with provisions set forth in the bylaws.

B. The same person may hold more than one office unless provided for otherwise in the bylaws.

C. An officer performs duties stated in the bylaws or by the board of directors or another officer to the extent consistent with the bylaws.

D. The secretary shall be responsible for preparing the records of any director or shareholder meeting.

V. REGISTERED AGENT

A. A corporation must register an agent with the state who has an office within the state.

VI. FILING FEES

A. Articles of Incorporation	$50.00
B. Change of Reg. Agent's Name/Address	$10.00
C. Application for Name Reservation	$10.00
D. Amending Articles of Incorporation	$10.00
E. Filing Annual Report	$30.00
F. Cost for Certified Copy of Any Document	$15.00

PENNSYLVANIA

Title 15, Pennsylvania Statutes
Department of State
Corporation Bureau
P. O. Box 8722
Harrisburg, PA 17105-8722
(717) 787-1057

I. ARTICLES OF INCORPORATION

A. Must be printed or typewritten in English.

B. Must provide state corporation office with the original copy of the Articles.

II. THE CORPORATE NAME

A. Name must contain the word "corporation", "incorporated", "company", "limited", "association", "fund", "syndicate" or abbreviation of the same.

B. Prior to incorporation, a corporate name may be reserved for a period of 120 days. Name must be reserved through written application, accompanied by docketing statement.

III. DIRECTORS

A. Directors need not be a resident of the commonwealth or a shareholder of the corporation.

B. The articles or bylaws may prescribe additional requirements or qualifications.

C. A corporation must have one director or more as initially stated in articles and thereafter as many directors as stated in bylaws.

D. Director(s) are normally elected at the annual meeting of shareholders.

IV. OFFICERS

A. A corporation must have a president, secretary and treasurer. Other officers may be elected or appointed in accordance with provisions set forth in the bylaws.

B. The same person may hold more than one office unless provided for otherwise in the bylaws.

C. An officer performs duties stated in the bylaws or by the board of directors to the extent consistent with the bylaws.

V. REGISTERED AGENT

A. Corporation need not have a registered agent, but must register with the state an office located in the state which can accept service of process.

VI. FILING FEES

A. Articles of Incorporation	$100.00
B. Change of Registered Agent's Name/Address	$52.00
C. Application for Name Reservation	$52.00
D. Amending Articles of Incorporation	$52.00
E. Cost for Certified Copy of Any Document	
	$28.00 + $12.00 search fee + $2.00/page

RHODE ISLAND

Title 7, General Laws of Rhode Island
Secretary of State
100 N. Main St.
Providence, RI 02903
(401) 277-3040

I. ARTICLES OF INCORPORATION

A. Must provide state corporation office with the original and one exact copy of the Articles.

II. CORPORATE NAME

A. Name must contain the word "corporation," "incorporated," "company," "limited" or abbreviation of the same.

B. Prior to incorporation, a corporate name may be reserved for a period of 120 days. Name availability may be requested over the telephone but may only be reserved through written application.

III. DIRECTORS

A. Directors need not be residents of the state or shareholders of the corporation.

B. The articles or bylaws may prescribe additional requirements or qualifications.

C. A corporation must have three directors or more as initially stated in articles and thereafter as many directors as stated in bylaws. However, when there are less than three shareholders, there need be only a corresponding number of directors.

D. Director(s) are normally elected at the annual meeting of shareholders.

IV. OFFICERS

A. A corporation must have a president and secretary. Other officers may be elected or appointed in accordance with provisions set forth in the bylaws.

B. The same person may hold more than one office unless provided for otherwise in the bylaws.

C. An officer performs duties stated in the bylaws or by the board of directors or another officer to the extent consistent with the bylaws.

V. REGISTERED AGENT

A. A corporation must register an agent with the state who has an office within the state.

VI. FILING FEES

A. Articles of Incorporation (up to 8,000 shares)	$150.00
B. Change of Registered Agent's Name/Address	$20.00
C. Application for Name Reservation	$50.00
D. Amending Articles of Incorporation	$50.00
E. Filing Annual Report	$50.00
F. Cost for Certified Copy of Any Document	
	$5.00 + .50 per page

SOUTH CAROLINA

Title 33, Code of Laws of South carolina

Secretary of State
P.O. Box 11350
Columbia, SC 29211
(803) 734-2158

I. ARTICLES OF INCORPORATION

A. Must be printed or typewritten in English.

B. Must provide state corporation office with the original and one exact copy of the Articles. The Articles must be signed by an incorporator, accompanied by a certificate stating that the requirements have been complied with and that the corporation is organized for a lawful and proper purpose, signed by an attorney licensed in South Carolina.

II. THE CORPORATE NAME

A. Name must contain the word "corporation", "incorporated", "company", "limited" or abbreviation of the same.

B. Prior to incorporation, a corporate name may be reserved for a period of 120 days. Name must be reserved through written application.

III. DIRECTORS

A. Directors need not be residents of the state or shareholders of the corporation.

B. The articles or bylaws may prescribe additional requirements or qualifications.

C. A corporation must have one director or more as initially stated in articles or bylaws.

D. Director(s) are normally elected at the annual meeting of shareholders.

IV. OFFICERS

A. A corporation must have the offices as described in the bylaws or as appointed by the board of directors in accordance with the bylaws.

B. The same person may hold more than one office unless provided for otherwise in the bylaws.

C. An officer performs duties stated in the bylaws or by the board of directors or another officer to the extent consistent with the bylaws.

D. One officer shall be responsible for preparing the records of any director or shareholder meeting.

V. REGISTERED AGENT

A. A corporation must register an agent with the state who has an office within the state.

VI. FILING FEES

A. Articles of Incorporation	$110.00*
B. Change of Registered Agent's Name/Address	$10.00
C. Application for Name Reservation	$10.00
D. Amending Articles of Incorporation	$110.00
E. Filing Annual Report (fee paid to Tax Commission)	$25.00
F. Cost for Certified Copy of Any Document	$2.00 + $.50/page

*Note: The fee includes a $10.00 filing fee and a $100.00 tax payable to the state treasurer.

SOUTH DAKOTA

Title 47, South Dakota Codified Laws

Secretary of State
State Capital
500 E. Capital Street
Pierre, SD 57501
(605) 773-3537

I. ARTICLES OF INCORPORATION

A. Must provide state corporation office with the original and one exact copy of the Articles.

B. Corporation cannot start business until the value of at least $1,000 has been received for the issuance of shares.

II. THE CORPORATE NAME

A. Name must contain the word "corporation", "incorporated", "company", "limited" or abbreviation of the same.

B. Prior to incorporation, a corporate name may be reserved for a period of 120 days. Name must be reserved through written application.

III. DIRECTORS

A. Directors need not be residents of the state or shareholders of the corporation.

B. The articles or bylaws may prescribe additional requirements or qualifications.

C. A corporation must have one director or more as initially stated in articles and thereafter as many directors as stated in bylaws.

D. Director(s) are normally elected at the annual meeting of shareholders.

IV. OFFICERS

A. A corporation shall have the officers described in its bylaws or appointed by the board in accordance with provisions set forth in the bylaws.

B. The same person may hold more than one office unless provided for otherwise in the bylaws.

C. An officer performs duties stated in the bylaws or by the board of directors or another officer to the extent consistent with the bylaws.

D. One officer shall be responsible for preparing the records of any director or shareholder meeting.

V. REGISTERED AGENT

A. A corporation must register an agent with the state who has an office within the state.

VI. FILING FEES

A. Articles of Incorporation (25,000 shares of stock or less)	$40.00
B. Change of Registered Agent's Name/Address	$5.00
C. Application for Name Reservation	$10.00
D. Amending Articles of Incorporation	$20.00
E. Filing Annual Report	$10.00
F. Cost for Certified Copy of Any Document	$5.00/certificate & .50/page

TENNESSEE

Title 48, Tennessee Code
Department of State
Division of Services
Suite 1800
James K. Polk Building
Nashville, TN 37243-0306
(615) 741-2286

I. CHARTER

A. Must provide state corporation office with the original and one exact copy of the Charter.

B. May need to file Articles in local county office where principal place of business will be located.

II. THE CORPORATE NAME

A. Name must contain the word "corporation", "incorporated", "company" or abbreviation of the same.

B. Prior to incorporation, a corporate name may be reserved for a period of 4 months. Name must be reserved through written application.

III. DIRECTORS

A. Directors need not be residents of the state or shareholders of the corporation.

B. The charter or bylaws may prescribe additional requirements or qualifications.

C. A corporation must have one director or more as initially stated in articles and thereafter as many directors as stated in bylaws.

D. Director(s) are normally elected at the annual meeting of shareholders.

IV. OFFICERS

A. A corporation must have a president and secretary. Other officers may be elected or appointed in accordance with provisions set forth in the bylaws.

B. The same person may hold more than one office unless provided for otherwise in the bylaws, except the offices of president and secretary.

C. An officer performs duties stated in the bylaws or by the board of directors or another officer to the extent consistent with the bylaws.

D. One officer shall be responsible for preparing the records of any director or shareholder meeting.

V. REGISTERED AGENT

A. A corporation must register an agent with the state who has an office within the state.

VI. FILING FEES

A. Charter (includes designation of initial office and agent)	$100.00
B. Application for Name Reservation	$20.00
C. Amending Articles of Incorporation	$20.00
D. Filing Annual Report	$20.00
E. Cost for Certified Copy of Any Document	$20.00

TEXAS

Business Corporation Act of Texas, Texas Civil Statutes
Secretary of State
Corporation Division
P.O. Box 13697
Austin, TX 78711
(512) 463-5555

I. ARTICLES OF INCORPORATION

A. Must provide state corporation office with the original and one exact copy of the Articles.

II. THE CORPORATE NAME

A. Name must contain the word "corporation", "incorporated", "company" or abbreviation of the same.

B. Prior to incorporation, a corporate name may be reserved for a period of 120 days. Name availability may be checked over the telephone, but may only be reserved through written application.

III. DIRECTORS

A. Directors need not be residents of the state or shareholders of the corporation.

B. The articles or bylaws may prescribe additional requirements or qualifications.

C. A corporation must have one director or more as initially stated in articles and thereafter as many directors as stated in bylaws.

D. Director(s) are normally elected at the annual meeting of shareholders.

IV. OFFICERS

A. A corporation must have a president and secretary. Other officers may be elected or appointed in accordance with provisions set forth in the bylaws.

B. The same person may hold more than one office unless provided for otherwise in the bylaws.

C. An officer performs duties stated in the bylaws or by the board of directors or another officer to the extent consistent with the bylaws.

V. REGISTERED AGENT

A. A corporation must register an agent with the state who has an office within the state.

VI. FILING FEES

A. Articles of Incorporation	$300.00
B. Change of Address of Registered Agent	$15.00
C. Application for Name Reservation	$40.00
D. Amending Articles of Incorporation	$150.00

UTAH

Title 16, Utah Code

    Department of Commerce
    Division of Corporations and Commercial Code
    P.O. Box 45801
    160 E. 300 South, 2nd Floor
    Salt Lake City, UT 84145-0801
    (801) 530-4849

I. ARTICLES OF INCORPORATION

A. Must provide state corporation office with the original and one exact copy of the Articles.

B. Three or more persons 18 years of age or older may act as incorporators.

II. THE CORPORATE NAME

A. Name must contain the word "corporation", "incorporated", "company" or abbreviation of the same.

B. Prior to incorporation, a corporate name may be reserved for a period of 120 days.

III. DIRECTORS

A. Directors need not be residents of the state or shareholders of the corporation.

B. The articles or bylaws may prescribe additional requirements or qualifications.

C. A corporation must have three directors or more as initially stated in articles and thereafter as many directors as stated in bylaws. However, when there are less than three shareholders, there need be only a corresponding number of directors.

D. Director(s) are normally elected at the annual meeting of shareholders.

IV. OFFICERS

A. A corporation must have at least one officer. Other officers may be elected or appointed in accordance with provisions set forth in the bylaws.

B. The same person may hold more than one office except for the offices of president and secretary.

C. An officer performs duties stated in the bylaws or by the board of directors to the extent consistent with the bylaws.

V. REGISTERED AGENT

A. A corporation must register an agent with the state who has an office within the state.

VI. FILING FEES

A. Articles of Incorporation	$50.00
B. Application for Name Reservation	$20.00
C. Amending Articles of Incorporation	$35.00
E. Filing Annual Report	$15.00
F. Cost for Certified Copy of Any Document	
	$10.00 + $.30/page

VERMONT

Title 11, Vermont Statutes

    Secretary of State
    109 State St.
    Montpelier, VT 05609-1104
    (802) 828-2363

I. ARTICLES OF ASSOCIATION

A. Must provide state corporation office with duplicate originals of the Articles.

B. At least one incorporator must be a resident of Vermont.

II. THE CORPORATE NAME

A. Name must contain the word "corporation", "incorporated", "company", "limited" or abbreviation of the same.

B. Prior to incorporation, a corporate name may be reserved for a period of 120 days. Name must be reserved through written application.

III. DIRECTORS

A. Directors need not be residents of the state or shareholders of the corporation.

B. The articles or bylaws may prescribe additional requirements or qualifications.

C. A corporation must have three directors or more as initially stated in articles and thereafter as many directors as stated in bylaws. However, when there are less than three shareholders, there need be only a corresponding number of directors.

D. Director(s) are normally elected at the annual meeting of shareholders.

IV. OFFICERS

A. A corporation must have a president, one or more vice presidents, a secretary and a treasurer. Other officers may be elected or appointed in accordance with provisions set forth in the bylaws. The secretary must be elected annually by the board.

B. The same person may hold more than one office unless provided for otherwise in the bylaws, except the offices of president and secretary.

C. An officer performs duties stated in the bylaws or by the board of directors.

D. The secretary shall be responsible for preparing the records of any director or shareholder meeting.

V. REGISTERED AGENT

A. A corporation must register an agent with the state who has an office within the state.

VI. FILING FEES

A. Articles of Incorporation (10,000 or less capital stock)	$35.00
B. Change of Registered Agent's Name/Address	$5.00
C. Application for Name Reservation	$10.00
D. Amending Articles of Incorporation	$25.00
E. Filing Annual Report	N/C
F. Cost for Certified Copy of Any Document	
	$5.00 + $1.00/page

VIRGINIA

Title 13, Code of Virginia
    State Corporation Commission
    Jefferson Building
    P.O. Box 1197
    Richmond, VA 23219
    (804) 371-9733

I.   ARTICLES OF INCORPORATION
    A.   Must be printed or typewritten in English.
    B.   Must provide state corporation office with the original and one exact copy of the Articles.

II.   THE CORPORATE NAME
    A.   Name must contain the word "corporation", "incorporated", "company", "limited" or abbreviation of the same.
    B.   Prior to incorporation, a corporate name may be reserved for a period of 120 days. Name availability may be checked by telephone but may only be reserved by written application.

III.   DIRECTORS
    A.   Directors need not be a resident of the commonwealth or a shareholder of the corporation.
    B.   The articles or bylaws may prescribe additional requirements or qualifications.
    C.   A corporation must have one director or more as initially stated in articles and thereafter as many directors as stated in bylaws. However, when there are less than three shareholders, there need be only a corresponding number of directors.
    D.   Director(s) are normally elected at the annual meeting of shareholders.

IV.   OFFICERS
    A.   A corporation must have a president and secretary. Other officers may be elected or appointed in accordance with provisions set forth in the bylaws.
    B.   The same person may hold more than one office unless provided for otherwise in the bylaws.
    C.   An officer performs duties stated in the bylaws or by the board of directors or another officer to the extent consistent with the bylaws.
    D.   The secretary shall be responsible for preparing the records of any director or shareholder meeting.

V.   REGISTERED AGENT
    A.   A corporation must register an agent with the state who has an office within the state.

VI.   FILING FEES

A. Articles of Incorporation (up to 25,000 shares of capital stock)	$75.00
B. Change of Registered Agent's Name/Address	$10.00
C. Application for Name Reservation	$10.00
D. Amending Articles of Incorporation	$25.00
E. Filing Annual Report	n/c
F. Cost for Certified Copy of Any Document	$1.00/page and $3.00/certificate

WASHINGTON

Title 23B, Revised Code of Washington
    Secretary of State
    Corporation Division
    P.O. Box 40234
    Olympia, WA 98504-0234
    (206) 753-7115

I.   ARTICLES OF INCORPORATION
    A.   Must be printed or typewritten in English.
    B.   Must provide state corporation office with the original and one exact copy of the Articles.

II.   THE CORPORATE NAME
    A.   Name must contain the word "corporation", "incorporated", "company", "limited" or abbreviation of the same.
    B.   Prior to incorporation, a corporate name may be reserved for a period of 180 days.

III.   DIRECTORS
    A.   Directors need not be residents of the state or shareholders of the corporation.
    B.   The articles or bylaws may prescribe additional requirements or qualifications.
    C.   A corporation must have one director or more with the number specified in or fixed in accordance with the articles or bylaws.
    D.   Director(s) are normally elected at the annual meeting of shareholders.

IV.   OFFICERS
    A.   A corporation must have the officers elected or appointed in accordance with provisions set forth in the bylaws.
    B.   The same person may hold more than one office unless provided for otherwise in the bylaws.
    C.   An officer performs duties stated in the bylaws or by the board of directors or another officer to the extent consistent with the bylaws.
    D.   One officer shall be responsible for preparing the records of any director or shareholder meeting.

V.   REGISTERED AGENT
    A.   A corporation must register an agent with the state who has an office within the state.
    B.   A consent must be filled with the Articles of Incorporation and may be worded as follows: I, _____, hereby consent to serve as Registered Agent in the state of Washington for the above named corporation. I understand that as agent for the corporation, it will be my responsibility to accept Service of Process on behalf of the corporation; to forward license renewals and other mail to the corporation; and to immediately notify the Office of the Secretary of State in the event of my resignation or of any changes in the Registered Office address.

(Signature of Registered Agent)
(Print Name and Title)
(Date)

VI.   FILING FEES

A. Articles of Incorporation	$175.00
B. Expedited service fee for fast filing	$10.00
C. Application for Name Reservation	$20.00
D. Amending Articles of Incorporation	$25.00
E. Filing Annual Report	$10.00
F. Cost for Certified Copy of Any Document	$10.00/certificate & .20/page
G. Annual License Fee	$60.00

WEST VIRGINIA

Chapter 13, West Virginia Code
    Secretary of State
    State Capital
    Charleston, WV 25305
    (304) 558-8000

I.   ARTICLES OF INCORPORATION
    A.   Must provide state corporation office with the original and one exact copy of the Articles.

II.   THE CORPORATE NAME
    A.   Name must contain the word "corporation", "incorporated", "company", "limited" or abbreviation of the same.
    B.   Prior to incorporation, a corporate name may be reserved for a period of 120 days. Name availability may be checked over the telephone, but must be reserved through written application.

III.   DIRECTORS
    A.   Directors need not be residents of the state or shareholders of the corporation.
    B.   The articles or bylaws may prescribe additional requirements or qualifications.
    C.   A corporation must have one director or more as initially stated in articles or bylaws.
    D.   Director(s) are normally elected at the annual meeting of shareholders.

IV.   OFFICERS
    A.   A corporation must have a president, secretary and treasurer. Other officers may be elected or appointed in accordance with provisions set forth in the bylaws.
    B.   The same person may hold more than one office, except those of president and secretary.
    C.   An officer performs duties stated in the bylaws or by the board of directors to the extent consistent with the bylaws.

V.   RESIDENT (REGISTERED) AGENT
    A.   Secretary of State accepts process for each corporation and he will mail process onto the corporation.

VI.   FILING FEES

A. Articles of Incorporation (up to 5000 shares of stock)	*$40.00
B. Application for Name Reservation	$5.00
C. Amending Articles of Incorporation	$5.00
D. Filing Annual Report	n/c
E. Cost for Certified Copy of Any Document	$10.00

* Filing fees may vary depending on the month the articles are filed. The actual fee for filing may range from $20.00 to $40.00.

WISCONSIN

Chapter 180, Wisconsin Statutes
    Secretary of State
    Corporation Division
    P.O. Box 7846
    Madison, WI 53707
    (608) 266-3590

I.   ARTICLES OF INCORPORATION
    A.   Articles must be written in English.
    B.   Must provide state corporation office with the original of the Articles.

II.   THE CORPORATE NAME
    A.   Name must contain the word "corporation", "incorporated", "company", "limited" or abbreviation of the same.
    B.   Prior to incorporation, a corporate name may be reserved for a period of 120 days. Name may be reserved through written or telephone application.

III.   DIRECTORS
    A.   Directors need not be residents of the state or shareholders of the corporation.
    B.   The articles or bylaws may prescribe additional requirements or qualifications.
    C.   A corporation must have one director or more as initially stated in articles.
    D.   Director(s) are normally elected at the annual meeting of shareholders.

IV.   OFFICERS
    A.   A corporation must have the officers as elected or appointed in accordance with provisions set forth in the bylaws.
    B.   The same person may hold more than one office unless provided for otherwise in the bylaws.
    C.   An officer performs duties stated in the bylaws or by the board of directors or another officer to the extent consistent with the bylaws.

V.   REGISTERED AGENT
    A.   A corporation must register an agent with the state who has an office within the state.

VI.   FILING FEES

A. Articles of Incorporation (up to 9000 shares for minimum fee)	$90.00
B. Change of Registered Agent's Name/Address	$10.00
C. Application for Name Reservation	$15.00
D. Telephone Application for Name Reservation	$30.00
E. Amending Articles of Incorporation	$40.00
F. Filing Annual Report	$25.00
G. Cost for Certified Copy of Any Document	$5.00 + $.50/page

WYOMING

Title 17, Wyoming Statutes
    Secretary of State
    State Capitol Building
    Cheyenne, WY 82002
    (307) 777-7311

I.   ARTICLES OF INCORPORATION
    A.   Must provide state corporation office with the original and one exact copy of the Articles.

II.   THE CORPORATE NAME
    A.   Name may not contain language stating or implying that the corporation is organized for an unlawful purpose.
    B.   Prior to incorporation, a corporate name may be reserved for a period of 120 days. Name availability may be checked over the telephone, but must be reserved through written application.

III.   DIRECTORS
    A.   Directors need not be residents of the state or shareholders of the corporation.
    B.   The articles or bylaws may prescribe additional requirements or qualifications.
    C.   A corporation must have one director or more as initially specified in or fixed in accordance with the articles or bylaws.
    D.   Director(s) are normally elected at the annual meeting of shareholders.

IV.   OFFICERS
    A.   A corporation has the officers as elected or appointed in accordance with provisions set forth in the bylaws.
    B.   The same person may hold more than one office unless provided for otherwise in the bylaws.
    C.   An officer performs duties stated in the bylaws or by the board of directors or another officer to the extent consistent with the bylaws.
    D.   One officer shall be responsible for preparing the records of any director or shareholder meeting.

V.   REGISTERED AGENT
    A.   A corporation must register an agent with the state who has an office within the state.

VI.   FILING FEES
    A. Articles of Incorporation $90.00
    B. Change of Registered Agent's Name/Address $20.00
    C. Application for Name Reservation $30.00
    D. Amending Articles of Incorporation $15.00
    E. Amending Articles of Incorporation to
         Change Corporate Name $45.00
    F. Filing Annual Report based on assets of corp.   n/c
    G. Cost for Certified Copy of Any Document
                      .50/1st 10 pages + $.15/page thereafter +
                                       $3.00 certification

Appendix B
State Incorporation Forms

Forms 1 through 7 are the forms which must be filed with the secretary of state to form a corporation.

Form 1 applies to the following states:

Alabama	Kansas	North Dakota
Alaska†	Kentucky	Ohio
Arizona	Maryland	Oregon
Arkansas	Michigan	Pennsylvania
California	Minnesota	Rhode Island
Colorado	Mississippi	South Carolina
District of Columbia	Missouri	Texas*
Florida	Montana	Utah*
Georgia	Nebraska	Virginia
Idaho	Nevada	Washington
Illinois	New Hampshire	West Virginia
Indiana	New Mexico	Wisconsin
Iowa	North Carolina	Wyoming

*For Texas and Utah, document must state: "The corporation will not commence business until $1,000 has been received for issuance of stock." (can be paid in money, labor, or property)

†For Alaska, the document must state: "The name and address of each alien affiliate is: (if none, please indicate N/A)"_____

               name   complete resident or business address

Form 2 applies to the following state:
Louisiana

Form 3 applies to the following states:
Delaware
Connecticut
New Jersey
New York
Oklahoma

Form 4 applies to the following states:
Maine
Massachusetts

Form 5 applies to the following state:
South Dakota

Form 6 applies to the following states:
Hawaii
Tennessee

Form 7 applies to the following state:
Vermont

STATE OF
_____

ARTICLES OF INCORPORATION
OF
_____,
A BUSINESS/STOCK CORPORATION

The name of the corporation is _____.

The business and mailing address of the corporation is_____
_____.
(street address, city, county, state, zip)

The duration of the corporation is perpetual.

The corporation has been organized to transact any and all lawful business for which corporations may be incorporated in this state.

The aggregate number of shares which the corporation shall have the authority to issue is_____ and the par value of each shall be _____ . (typically "no par value")

The number of directors constituting the initial board of directors of the corporation is _____, and their names and addresses are:

The location and street address of the initial registered office is _____
_____ (must be located within the state) (list county also)
and the name of its initial registered agent at such address is _____

The name and address of each incorporator:

In witness thereof, the undersigned incorporator(s) have executed these articles of incorporation this ____ day of _____, 19_____.

_____   _____
Witness   Incorporator

_____   _____
Witness   Incorporator

State of _____
County of_____

On _____, the above person(s) appeared before me, a notary public and are personally known or proved to me to be the person(s) whose name(s) is/are subscribed to the above instrument who acknowledged that he/she executed the instrument.

_____
Notary

(Notary stamp or seal)

This document prepared by:

_____

Consent of Appointment by the Registered Agent

I, _____, hereby give my consent to serve as the registered agent for
     (name of registered agent)

_____.
     (corporate name)

Dated_____, 19_____.

                                          _____
                                          (signature of registered agent)

Articles prepared by:

STATE OF
_____

ARTICLES OF INCORPORATION
OF
_____ ,

A BUSINESS/STOCK CORPORATION

The name of the corporation is _____.

The business and mailing address of the corporation is _____
_____
              (street address, city, county, state, zip)

The duration of the corporation is perpetual.

The corporation has been organized to transact any and all lawful business for which corporations may be incorporated in this state.

The aggregate number of shares which the corporation shall have the authority to issue is_____ and the par value of each shall be _____ **(typically "no par value")**

The location and street address of the initial registered office is _____
_____ **(must be located within the state) (list county also)**
and the name of its initial registered agent at such address is_____.

The corporation's federal tax identification number is
The name and address of each incorporator:

In witness thereof, the undersigned incorporator(s) have executed these articles of incorporation this _____ day of _____, 19_____ .

_____
Witness

_____
Witness

_____
Witness

_____
Incorporator

_____
Incorporator

_____
Incorporator

State of _____
County of _____

On_____ , the above person(s) appeared before me, a notary public, and are personally known or proved to me to be the person(s) whose name(s) is/are subscribed to the above instrument who acknowledged that he/she executed the instrument.

_____
Notary

(Notary stamp or seal)

This document prepared by:

STATE OF
_____

CERTIFICATE OF INCORPORATION
OF
_____ ,

A BUSINESS/STOCK CORPORATION

The name of the corporation is _____ .

The business and mailing address of the corporation is _____
_____
                (street address, city, county, state, zip)

The duration of the corporation is perpetual.

The corporation has been organized to transact any and all lawful business for which corporations may be incorporated in this state.

The aggregate number of shares which the corporation shall have the authority to issue is_____ and the par value of each shall be _____ (typically "no par value")

The amount of the total authorized capitalized stock of this corporation is_____ Dollars ($_____) divided into _____ shares, of _____ Dollars ($_____).

The number of directors constituting the initial board of directors of the corporation is _____ , and their names and addresses are:

The location and street address of the initial registered office is _____
_____ **(must be located within the state) (list county also)**
and the name of its initial registered agent at such address is_____ .

The name and address of each incorporator:

In witness thereof, the undersigned incorporator(s) have executed this certificate of incorporation this _____ day of _____ , 19____ .

_____
Incorporator

_____
Incorporator

State of _____
County of _____

On_____ , the above person(s) appeared before me, a notary public and are personally known or proved to me to be the person(s) whose name(s) is/are subscribed to the above instrument who acknowledged that he/she executed the instrument.

_____
Notary

(Notary stamp or seal)

This document prepared by:

STATE OF
_____

ARTICLES OF INCORPORATION
OF
_____ ,

A BUSINESS/STOCK CORPORATION

The name of the corporation is _____.

The business and mailing address of the corporation is _____
_____
            (street address, city, county, state, zip)
The duration of the corporation is perpetual.

The corporation has been organized to transact any and all lawful business for which corporations may be incorporated in this state.

The aggregate number of shares which the corporation shall have the authority to issue is_____ and the par value of each shall be _____ **(typically "no par value")**

The number of directors constituting the initial board of directors of the corporation is ____ , and their names and addresses are:

The location and street address of the initial registered office is _____
_____ **(must be located within the state) (list county also)**
and the name of its initial registered agent at such address is_____.

The fiscal year shall be_____

The name and address of each officer:

Title	Name	Address
PRESIDENT		
TREASURER		
CLERK		

The name and address of each incorporator:

In witness thereof, the undersigned incorporator(s) have executed these articles of incorporation this _____ day of _____, 19____.

_____
Incorporator

_____
Incorporator

State of _____
County of _____

On_____ , the above person(s) appeared before me, a notary public and are personally known or proved to me to be the person(s) whose name(s) is/are subscribed to the above instrument who acknowledged that he/she executed the instrument.

_____
Notary

(Notary stamp or seal)
This document prepared by:

STATE OF
_____

ARTICLES OF INCORPORATION
OF
_____ ,
A BUSINESS/STOCK CORPORATION

The name of the corporation is _____.

The business and mailing address of the corporation is _____
_____ (street address, city, county, state, zip)

The corporation has been organized to transact any and all lawful business for which corporations may be incorporated in this state.

The names of the initial subscribers for shares, the number of shares subscribed for, the subscription price and the amount of capital paid are as follows:

Name of initial subscribers:
1.
2.
3.

Number of shares subscribed for by each corresponding subscriber:
1.
2.
3.

Subscription price for the shares subscribed for by each subscriber:
1.
2.
3.

Amount of capital paid in cash by each subscriber:
1.
2.
3.

The name and address of each incorporator:

In witness thereof, the undersigned incorporator(s) have executed these articles of incorporation this _____ day of _____, 19____.

_____
Incorporator

_____
Incorporator

State of _____
County of _____

On_____ , the above person(s) appeared before me, a notary public and are personally known or proved to me to be the person(s) whose name(s) is/are subscribed to the above instrument who acknowledged that he/she executed the instrument.

_____
Notary

(Notary stamp or seal)
This document prepared by:

STATE OF

_____

CHARTER
OF

_____ ,

A BUSINESS/STOCK CORPORATION

The name of the corporation is _____.

The business and mailing address of the corporation is _____
_____ (street address, city, county, state, zip)

The duration of the corporation is perpetual.

The corporation has been organized to transact any and all lawful business for which corporations may be incorporated in this state.

The aggregate number of shares which the corporation shall have the authority to issue is_____ and the par value of each shall be _____ (typically "no par value")

The corporation will not commence business until consideration of the value of at least One Thousand Dollars ($1,000.00) has been received for the issuance of shares.

The number of directors constituting the initial board of directors of the corporation is _____, and their names and addresses are:

The location and street address of the initial registered office is _____
_____ (must be located within the state) (list county also)
and the name of its initial registered agent at such address is_____.

The corporation's federal tax identification number is _____

The fiscal year shall be _____

The name and address of each officer:

Title	Name	Address

The name and address of each incorporator:

In witness thereof, the undersigned incorporator(s) have executed this charter this _____ day of
_____, 19____.

_____
Incorporator

_____
Incorporator

State of _____

County of _____

On_____ , the above person(s) appeared before me, a notary public and are personally known or proved to me to be the person(s) whose name(s) is/are subscribed to the above instrument who acknowledged that he/she executed the instrument.

_____
Notary

(Notary stamp or seal)

_____

Consent of Appointment by the Registered Agent

I, _____, hereby give my consent to serve as the registered agent for
   (name of registered agent)

_____.
                    (corporate name)

Dated_____, 19_____.

_____
(signature of registered agent)

Articles prepared by:

ARTICLES OF ASSOCIATION

The name of the corporation shall be...

The initial registered agent shall be...

(NOTE: A Corporation CANNOT be its own registered agent)

with registered agent's address at...

| Box # | Street | Town | State | Zip |

The corporation shall be located at...

| Box # | Street | Town | State | Zip |

The operating year shall be: Calendar........................Fiscal...

(Dec. 31)   (Month-Day)

If a fiscal year ending is not specified, the calendar year ending December 31st shall be designated as your fiscal year ending.

The period of duration shall be (if not perpetual, so state)...

Please check appropriate box:

☐ Vermont General Corporation (T. 11, Ch. 17)　☐ Worker Cooperative (T. 11, Ch. 8)

☐ Vermont Professional Corporation (T.11, Ch. 3)　☐ Cooperative Marketing Act (T.11, Ch. 7)

☐ Vermont Non-Profit Corporation (T.11, Ch. 19)　☐ Cooperative Housing Ownership Act (T.11, Ch. 14)

This corporation is organized for the purpose of:

Here set out purpose
clearly and briefly,
using separate paragraphs
to cover each
seperate purpose.

EACH VERMONT CORPORATION MUST FILE AN ANNUAL REPORT WITHIN TWO AND ONE HALF (2 1/2) MONTHS AFTER THE EXPIRATION OF ITS FISCAL YEAR ENDING.

The following information regarding shares must be completed by business corporations. **Non-profit corporations cannot have shares.**

The aggregate number of shares the corporation shall have authority to issue is

........................shares, common, with a par value of (if no par value, so state)$...

........................shares, preferred, with a par value of (if no par value, so state)$...

If preferred shares are provided
for, state here briefly the terms
of preference.
If shares are to be divided into
classes or series, state here the
designations, preferences, limitations,
and relative rights of each class
or series.

Directors: Business corporations with three or more shareholders must have at least three directors. If there are fewer than three shareholders, the number of directors may be equal to, **but not less than,** the number of shareholders.

Non-profit corporations must have at least three directors.

The initial board of directors shall have................................members with the following serving as directors until their successors are elected and qualify:

If fewer than three directors are named, then the number of shareholders can not exceed the number of directors.

Directors:	*Address:*			
	Street	Town	State	Zip

Dated at..., in the County of...

this...day of..., 19.................

Each Incorporator must sign	Residence of each Incorporator			
	Street	Town	State	Zip

(one or more persons may act as incorporators, at least one of whom shall reside in Vermont.)

Names must be **Printed or Typed** under all signatures.

IN ADDITION TO ALL THE PRECEDING INFORMATION, VERMONT PROFESSIONAL CORPORATIONS MUST COMPLETE THE CERTIFICATE ON THE LAST PAGE OF THIS APPLICATION.

Appendix C
Corporate Forms

94

_____
(date)

_____
_____
_____
_____

Dear Sir or Madam:

Enclosed please find the necessary documents for the corporate registration of_____, along with a check in the amount of $_____ for the filing fee and any other required costs.

Also enclosed is a photocopy of the these corporate documents. Please return this to me with the filing date stamped on it.

Thank you,

_____

Form SS-4
Application for Employer Identification Number

(Rev. April 1991)
Department of the Treasury
Internal Revenue Service

(For use by employers and others. Please read the attached instructions before completing this form.)

EIN

OMB No. 1545-0003
Expires 4-30-94

Please type or print clearly.

1 Name of applicant (True legal name) (See instructions.)

2 Trade name of business, if different from name in line 1

3 Executor, trustee, "care of" name

4a Mailing address (street address) (room, apt., or suite no.)

5a Address of business (See instructions.)

4b City, state, and ZIP code

5b City, state, and ZIP code

6 County and state where principal business is located

7 Name of principal officer, grantor, or general partner (See instructions.) ▶

8a Type of entity (Check only one box.) (See instructions.)
- [ ] Individual SSN _____
- [ ] REMIC
- [ ] State/local government
- [ ] Personal service corp.
- [ ] National guard
- [ ] Other nonprofit organization (specify) _____ If nonprofit organization enter GEN (if applicable) _____
- [ ] Other (specify) ▶
- [ ] Estate
- [ ] Plan administrator SSN _____
- [ ] Other corporation (specify) _____
- [ ] Federal government/military
- [ ] Trust
- [ ] Partnership
- [ ] Farmers' cooperative
- [ ] Church or church controlled organization

8b If a corporation, give name of foreign country (if applicable) or state in the U.S. where incorporated ▶

Foreign country

State

9 Reason for applying (Check only one box.)
- [ ] Started new business
- [ ] Hired employees
- [ ] Created a pension plan (specify type) ▶
- [ ] Banking purpose (specify) ▶
- [ ] Changed type of organization (specify) ▶ _____
- [ ] Purchased going business
- [ ] Created a trust (specify) ▶ _____
- [ ] Other (specify) ▶

10 Date business started or acquired (Mo., day, year) (See instructions.)

11 Enter closing month of accounting year. (See instructions.)

12 First date wages or annuities were paid or will be paid (Mo., day, year). **Note:** *If applicant is a withholding agent, enter date income will first be paid to nonresident alien. (Mo., day, year)* . . . . ▶

13 Enter highest number of employees expected in the next 12 months. **Note:** *If the applicant does not expect to have any employees during the period, enter "0."* . . . . . . ▶

Nonagricultural	Agricultural	Household

14 Principal activity (See instructions.) ▶

15 Is the principal business activity manufacturing? . . . . [ ] Yes [ ] No
If "Yes," principal product and raw material used ▶

16 To whom are most of the products or services sold? Please check the appropriate box.   [ ] Business (wholesale)
- [ ] Public (retail)
- [ ] Other (specify) ▶
- [ ] N/A

17a Has the applicant ever applied for an identification number for this or any other business? . . . . [ ] Yes [ ] No
Note: *If "Yes," please complete lines 17b and 17c.*

17b If you checked the "Yes" box in line 17a, give applicant's true name and trade name, if different than name shown on prior application.

True name ▶

Trade name ▶

17c Enter approximate date, city, and state where the application was filed and the previous employer identification number if known.

Approximate date when filed (Mo., day, year)	City and state where filed	Previous EIN

Under penalties of perjury, I declare that I have examined this application, and to the best of my knowledge and belief, it is true, correct, and complete

Telephone number (include area code)

Name and title (Please type or print clearly.) ▶

Signature ▶

Date ▶

Note: *Do not write below this line.   For official use only.*

Please leave blank ▶	Geo.	Ind.	Class	Size	Reason for applying

For Paperwork Reduction Act Notice, see attached instructions.

Cat. No. 16055N

Form **SS-4** (Rev. 4-91)

General Instructions

(Section references are to the Internal Revenue Code unless otherwise noted.)

Paperwork Reduction Act Notice.—We ask for the information on this form to carry out the Internal Revenue laws of the United States. You are required to give us this information. We need it to ensure that you are complying with these laws and to allow us to figure and collect the right amount of tax.

The time needed to complete and file this form will vary depending on individual circumstances. The estimated average time is:

Recordkeeping	7 min.
Learning about the law or the form	21 min.
Preparing the form	42 min.
Copying, assembling, and sending the form to IRS	20 min.

If you have comments concerning the accuracy of these time estimates or suggestions for making this form more simple, we would be happy to hear from you. You can write to both the **Internal Revenue Service,** Washington, DC 20224, Attention: IRS Reports Clearance Officer, T:FP; and the **Office of Management and Budget,** Paperwork Reduction Project (1545-0003), Washington, DC 20503. **DO NOT** send the tax form to either of these offices. Instead, see **Where To Apply.**

Purpose.—Use Form SS-4 to apply for an employer identification number (EIN). The information you provide on this form will establish your filing requirements.

Who Must File.—You must file this form if you have not obtained an EIN before and

- You pay wages to one or more employees.
- You are required to have an EIN to use on any return, statement, or other document, even if you are not an employer.
- You are required to withhold taxes on income, other than wages, paid to a nonresident alien (individual, corporation, partnership, etc.). For example, individuals who file **Form 1042,** Annual Withholding Tax Return for U.S. Source Income of Foreign Persons, to report alimony paid to nonresident aliens must have EINs.

Individuals who file **Schedule C,** Profit or Loss From Business, or **Schedule F,** Profit or Loss From Farming, of **Form 1040,** U.S. Individual Income Tax Return, must use EINs if they have a Keogh plan or are required to file excise, employment, or alcohol, tobacco, or firearms returns.

The following must use EINs even if they do not have any employees:

- Trusts, except an IRA trust, unless the IRA trust is required to file **Form 990-T,** Exempt Organization Business Income Tax Return, to report unrelated business taxable income or is filing Form 990-T to obtain a refund of the credit from a regulated investment company.
- Estates
- Partnerships
- REMICS (real estate mortgage investment conduits)
- Corporations
- Nonprofit organizations (churches, clubs, etc.)
- Farmers' cooperatives
- Plan administrators

*New Business.—*If you become the new owner of an existing business, **DO NOT** use the EIN of the former owner. If you already have an EIN, use that number. If you do not have an EIN, apply for one on this form. If you become the "owner" of a corporation by acquiring its stock, use the corporation's EIN.

If you already have an EIN, you may need to get a new one if either the organization or ownership of your business changes. If you incorporate a sole proprietorship or form a partnership, you must get a new EIN. However, **DO NOT** apply for a new EIN if you change only the name of your business.

File Only One Form SS-4.—File only one Form SS-4, regardless of the number of businesses operated or trade names under which a business operates. However, each corporation in an affiliated group must file a separate application.

If you do not have an EIN by the time a return is due, write "Applied for" and the date you applied in the space shown for the number. **DO NOT** show your social security number as an EIN on returns.

If you do not have an EIN by the time a tax deposit is due, send your payment to the Internal Revenue service center for your filing area. (See **Where To Apply** below.) Make your check or money order payable to Internal Revenue Service and show your name (as shown on Form SS-4), address, kind of tax, period covered, and date you applied for an EIN.

For more information about EINs, see **Pub. 583,** Taxpayers Starting a Business.

How To Apply.—You can apply for an EIN either by mail or by telephone. You can get an EIN immediately by calling the Tele-TIN phone number for the service center for your state, or you can send the completed Form SS-4 directly to the service center to receive your EIN in the mail.

*Application by Tele-TIN.—*The Tele-TIN program is designed to assign EINs by telephone. Under this program, you can receive your EIN over the telephone and use it immediately to file a return or make a payment.

To receive an EIN by phone, complete Form SS-4, then call the Tele-TIN phone number listed for your state under **Where To Apply.** The person making the call must be authorized to sign the form (see **Signature block** on page 3).

An IRS representative will use the information from the Form SS-4 to establish your account and assign you an EIN. Write the number you are given on the upper right-hand corner of the form, sign and date it, and promptly mail it to the Tele-TIN Unit at the service center address for your state.

*Application by mail.—*Complete Form SS-4 at least 4 to 5 weeks before you will need an EIN. Sign and date the application and mail it to the service center address for your state. You will receive your EIN in the mail in approximately 4 weeks.

Note: *The Tele-TIN phone numbers listed below will involve a long-distance charge to callers outside of the local calling area, and should only be used to apply for an EIN. Use 1-800-829-1040 to ask about an application by mail.*

Where To Apply.—

If your principal business, office or agency, or legal residence in the case of an individual, is located in:	Call the Tele-TIN phone number shown or file with the Internal Revenue service center at:
Florida, Georgia, South Carolina	Atlanta, GA 39901 (404) 455-2360
New Jersey, New York City and counties of Nassau, Rockland, Suffolk, and Westchester	Holtsville, NY 00501 (516) 447-4955
New York (all other counties), Connecticut, Maine, Massachusetts, New Hampshire, Rhode Island, Vermont	Andover, MA 05501 (508) 474-9717
Illinois, Iowa, Minnesota, Missouri, Wisconsin	Kansas City, MO 64999 (816) 926-5999
Delaware, District of Columbia, Maryland, Pennsylvania, Virginia	Philadelphia, PA 19255 (215) 961-3980
Indiana, Kentucky, Michigan, Ohio, West Virginia	Cincinnati, OH 45999 (606) 292-5467
Kansas, New Mexico, Oklahoma, Texas	Austin, TX 73301 (512) 462-7845
Alaska, Arizona, California (counties of Alpine, Amador, Butte, Calaveras, Colusa, Contra Costa, Del Norte, El Dorado, Glenn, Humboldt, Lake, Lassen, Marin, Mendocino, Modoc, Napa, Nevada, Placer, Plumas, Sacramento, San Joaquin, Shasta, Sierra, Siskiyou, Solano, Sonoma, Sutter, Tehama, Trinity, Yolo, and Yuba), Colorado, Idaho, Montana, Nebraska, Nevada, North Dakota, Oregon, South Dakota, Utah, Washington, Wyoming	Ogden, UT 84201 (801) 625-7645
California (all other counties), Hawaii	Fresno, CA 93888 (209) 456-5900
Alabama, Arkansas, Louisiana, Mississippi, North Carolina, Tennessee	Memphis, TN 37501 (901) 365-5970

If you have no legal residence, principal place of business, or principal office or agency in any Internal Revenue District, file your form with the Internal Revenue Service Center, Philadelphia, PA 19255 or call (215) 961-3980.

Specific Instructions

The instructions that follow are for those items that are not self-explanatory. Enter N/A (nonapplicable) on the lines that do not apply.

Line 1.—Enter the legal name of the entity applying for the EIN.

*Individuals.—*Enter the first name, middle initial, and last name.

*Trusts.—*Enter the name of the trust.

*Estate of a decedent.—*Enter the name of the estate.

*Partnerships.—*Enter the legal name of the partnership as it appears in the partnership agreement.

*Corporations.—*Enter the corporate name as set forth in the corporation charter or other legal document creating it.

*Plan administrators.—*Enter the name of the plan administrator. A plan administrator who already has an EIN should use that number.

Line 2.—Enter the trade name of the business if different from the legal name.

Note: *Use the full legal name entered on line 1 on all tax returns to be filed for the entity. However, if a trade name is entered on line 2, use only the name on line 1 or the name on line 2 consistently when filing tax returns.*

Line 3.—Trusts enter the name of the trustee. Estates enter the name of the executor, administrator, or other fiduciary. If the entity applying has a designated person to receive tax information, enter that person's name as the "care of" person. Print or type the first name, middle initial, and last name.

Lines 5a and 5b.—If the physical location of the business is different from the mailing address (lines 4a and 4b), enter the address of the physical location on lines 5a and 5b.

Line 7.—Enter the first name, middle initial, and last name of a principal officer if the business is a corporation; of a general partner if a partnership; and of a grantor if a trust.

Line 8a.—Check the box that best describes the type of entity that is applying for the EIN. If not specifically mentioned, check the "other" box and enter the type of entity. Do not enter N/A.

Individual.—Check this box if the individual files Schedule C or F (Form 1040) and has a Keogh plan or is required to file excise, employment, or alcohol, tobacco, or firearms returns. If this box is checked, enter the individual's SSN (social security number) in the space provided.

Plan administrator.—The term plan administrator means the person or group of persons specified as the administrator by the instrument under which the plan is operated. If the plan administrator is an individual, enter the plan administrator's SSN in the space provided.

New withholding agent.—If you are a new withholding agent required to file Form 1042, check the "other" box and enter in the space provided "new withholding agent."

REMICs.—Check this box if the entity is a real estate mortgage investment conduit (REMIC). A REMIC is any entity

1. To which an election to be treated as a REMIC applies for the tax year and all prior tax years,

2. In which all of the interests are regular interests or residual interests,

3. Which has one class of residual interests (and all distributions, if any, with respect to such interests are pro rata,

4. In which as of the close of the 3rd month beginning after the startup date and at all times thereafter, substantially all of its assets consist of qualified mortgages and permitted investments,

5. Which has a tax year that is a calendar year, and

6. With respect to which there are reasonable arrangements designed to ensure that: (a) residual interests are not held by disqualified organizations (as defined in section 860E(e)(5)), and (b) information necessary for the application of section 860E(e) will be made available.

For more information about REMICs see the Instructions for **Form 1066,** U. S. Real Estate Mortgage Investment Conduit Income Tax Return.

Personal service corporations.—Check this box if the entity is a personal service corporation. An entity is a personal service corporation for a tax year only if

1. The entity is a C corporation for the tax year.

2. The principal activity of the entity during the testing period (as defined in Temporary Regulations section 1.441-4T(f)) for the tax year is the performance of personal service.

3. During the testing period for the tax year, such services are substantially performed by employee-owners.

4. The employee-owners own 10 percent of the fair market value of the outstanding stock in the entity on the last day of the testing period for the tax year.

For more information about personal service corporations, see the instructions to **Form 1120,** U.S. Corporation Income Tax Return, and Temporary Regulations section 1.441-4T.

Other corporations.—This box is for any corporation other than a personal service corporation. If you check this box, enter the type of corporation (such as insurance company) in the space provided.

Other nonprofit organizations.—Check this box if the nonprofit organization is other than a church or church-controlled organization and specify the type of nonprofit organization (for example, an educational organization.)

Group exemption number (GEN).—If the applicant is a nonprofit organization that is a subordinate organization to be included in a group exemption letter under Revenue Procedure 80-27, 1980-1 C.B. 677, enter the GEN in the space provided. If you do not know the GEN, contact the parent organization for it. GEN is a four-digit number. Do not confuse it with the nine-digit EIN.

Line 9.—Check only one box. Do not enter N/A.

Started new business.—Check this box if you are starting a new business that requires an EIN. If you check this box, enter the type of business being started. **DO NOT** apply if you already have an EIN and are only adding another place of business.

Changed type of organization.—Check this box if the business is changing its type of organization, for example, if the business was a sole proprietorship and has been incorporated or has become a partnership. If you check this box, specify in the space provided the type of change made, for example, "from sole proprietorship to partnership."

Purchased going business.—Check this box if you acquired a business through purchase. Do not use the former owner's EIN. If you already have an EIN, use that number.

Hired employees.—Check this box if the existing business is requesting an EIN because it has hired or is hiring employees and is therefore required to file employment tax return for which an EIN is required. **DO NOT** apply if you already have an EIN and are only hiring employees.

Created a trust.—Check this box if you created a trust, and enter the type of trust created.

Created a pension plan.—Check this box if you have created a pension plan and need this number for reporting purposes. Also, enter the type of plan created.

Banking purpose.—Check this box if you are requesting an EIN for banking purpose only and enter the banking purpose (for example, checking, loan, etc.).

Other (specify).—Check this box if you are requesting an EIN for any reason other than those for which there are checkboxes and enter the reason.

Line 10.—If you are starting a new business, enter the starting date of the business. If the business you acquired is already operating, enter the date you acquired the business. Trusts should enter the date the trust was legally created. Estates should enter the date of death of the decedent whose name appears on line 1.

Line 11.—Enter the last month of your accounting year or tax year. An accounting year or tax year is usually 12 consecutive months. It may be a calendar year or a fiscal year (including a period of 52 or 53 weeks). A calendar year is 12 consecutive months ending on December 31. A fiscal year is either 12 consecutive months ending on the last day of any month other than December or a 52-53 week year. For more information

on accounting periods, see **Pub. 538,** Accounting Periods and Methods.

Individuals.—Your tax year generally will be a calendar year.

Partnerships.—Partnerships generally should conform to the tax year of either (1) its majority partners; (2) its principal partners; (3) the tax year that results in the least aggregate deferral of income (see Temporary Regulations section 1.706-1T); or (4) some other tax year, if (a) a business purpose is established for the fiscal year, or (b) the fiscal year is a "grandfather" year, or (c) an election is made under section 444 to have a fiscal year. (See the Instructions for **Form 1065,** U.S. Partnership Return of Income, for more information.)

REMICs.—Remics must have a calendar year as their tax year.

Personal service corporations.—A personal service corporation generally must adopt a calendar year unless:

1. It can establish to the satisfaction of the Commissioner that there is a business purpose for having a different tax year, or

2. It elects under section 444 to have a tax year other than a calendar year.

Line 12.—If the business has or will have employees, enter on this line the date on which the business began or will begin to pay wages to the employees. If the business does not have any plans to have employees, enter N/A on this line.

New withholding agent.—Enter the date you began or will begin to pay income to a nonresident alien. This also applies to individuals who are required to file Form 1042 to report alimony paid to a nonresident alien.

Line 14.—Generally, enter the exact type of business being operated (for example, advertising agency, farm, labor union, real estate agency, steam laundry, rental of coin-operated vending machine, investment club, etc.).

Governmental.—Enter the type of organization (state, county, school district, or municipality, etc.)

Nonprofit organization (other than governmental).—Enter whether organized for religious, educational, or humane purposes, and the principal activity (for example, religious organization—hospital, charitable).

Mining and quarrying.—Specify the process and the principal product (for example, mining bituminous coal; contract drilling for oil, quarrying dimension stone, etc.).

Contract construction.—Specify whether general contracting or special trade contracting. Also, show the type of work normally performed (for example, general contractor for residential buildings, electrical subcontractor, etc.).

Trade.—Specify the type of sales and the principal line of goods sold (for example, wholesale dairy products, manufacturer's representative for mining machinery, retail hardware, etc.).

Manufacturing.—Specify the type of establishment operated (for example, sawmill, vegetable cannery, etc.).

Signature block.—The application must be signed by: (1) the individual, if the person is an individual, (2) the president, vice president, or other principal officer, if the person is a corporation, (3) a responsible and duly authorized member or officer having knowledge of its affairs, if the person is a partnership or other unincorporated organization, or (4) the fiduciary, if the person is a trust or estate.

100

WAIVER OF NOTICE

OF THE ORGANIZATION MEETING

OF

_____

        We, the undersigned incorporators named in the certificate of
incorporation of the above-named corporation hereby agree and consent
that the organization meeting of the corporation be held on the date
and time and place stated below and hereby waive all notice of such
meeting and of any adjournment thereof.

Place of meeting: _____

Date of Meeting: _____

Time of meeting: _____

Dated: _____

                                    _____
                                    Incorporator

                                    _____
                                    Incorporator

                                    _____
                                    Incorporator

MINUTES OF THE ORGANIZATIONAL MEETING OF

INCORPORATORS AND DIRECTORS OF

_____

The organization meeting of the above corporation was held on
_____, 19____ at _____
_____ at _____ o'clock ___m.

The following persons were present:

_____   _____
_____   _____
_____   _____

The Waiver of notice of this meeting was signed by all directors
and incorporators named in the Articles of Incorporation and filed in
the minute book.

The meeting was called to order by _____
an Incorporator named in the Articles of Incorporation.
_____ was nominated and elected Chairman and acted as such
until relieved by the president. _____ was
nominated and elected temporary secretary, and acted as such until
relieved by the permanent secretary.

A copy of the Articles of Incorporation which was filed with the
Secretary of State of the State of _____ on
_____, 19____ was examined by the Directors and
Incorporators and filed in the minute book.

The election of officers for the coming year was then held and
the following were duly nominated and elected by the Board of Directors
to be the officers of the corporation, to serve until such time as their
successors are elected and qualified:

President: _____
Vice President: _____
Secretary: _____
Treasurer: _____

The proposed Bylaws for the corporation were then presented to
the meeting and discussed. Upon motion duly made, seconded and carried,
the Bylaws were adopted and added to the minute book.

A corporate seal for the corporation was then presented to the meeting and upon motion duly made, seconded and carried, it was adopted as the seal of the corporation. An impression thereof was then made in the margin of these minutes

The necessity of opening a bank account was then discussed and upon motion duly made, seconded and carried, the following resolution was adopted:

RESOLVED that the corporation open bank accounts with _____ _____ and that the officers of the corporation are authorized to take such action as is necessary to open such accounts; that the bank's printed form of resolution is hereby adopted and incorporated into these minutes by reference and shall be placed in the minute book; that any ____ of the following persons shall have signature authority over the account:

_____   _____
_____   _____
_____   _____

Proposed stock certificates and stock transfer ledger were then presented to the meeting and examined. Upon motion duly made, seconded and carried the stock certificates and ledger were adopted as the certificates and transfer book to be used by the corporation. A sample stock certificate marked "VOID" and the stock transfer ledger were then added to the minute book. Upon motion duly made, seconded and carried, it was then resolved that the stock certificates, when issued, would be signed by the President and the Secretary of the corporation.

The tax status of the corporation was then discussed and it was moved, seconded and carried that the stock of the corporation be issued under §1244 of the Internal Revenue Code and that the officers of the corporation take the necessary action to:

1.   Obtain an employer tax number by filing form SS-4,

2.   ☐ Become an S-Corporation for tax purposes,
      ☐ Remain a C-Corporation for tax purposes,

The expenses of organizing the corporation were then discussed and it was moved, seconded and carried that the corporation pay in full from the corporate funds the expenses and reimburse any advances made by the incorporators upon proof of payment.

The Directors named in the Articles of Incorporation then tendered their resignations, effective upon the adjournment of this meeting. Upon motion duly made, seconded and carried, the following named persons were elected as Directors of the corporation, each to hold office until the first annual meeting of shareholders, and until a successor of each shall have been elected and qualified.

_____
_____
_____

There were presented to the corporation, the following offer(s) to purchase shares of capital stock:

FROM	NO. OF SHARES	CONSIDERATION
_____	_____	_____
_____	_____	_____
_____	_____	_____
_____	_____	_____

The offers were discussed and after motion duly made, seconded and carried were approved. It was further resolved that the Board of Directors has determined that the consideration was valued at least equal to the value of the shares to be issued and that upon tender of the consideration, fully paid non-assessable shares of the corporation be issued.

There being no further business before the meeting, on motion duly made, seconded and carried, the meeting adjourned.

DATED: _____

_____
President

_____
Secretary

BYLAWS OF

A _____ CORPORATION

ARTICLE I - OFFICES

The principal office of the Corporation shall be located in the City of _____ and the State of _____. The Corporation may also maintain offices at such other places as the Board of Directors may, from time to time, determine.

ARTICLE II - SHAREHOLDERS

Section 1 - Annual Meetings: The annual meeting of the shareholders of the Corporation shall be held each year on _____ at _____m. at the principal office of the Corporation or at such other places, within or without the State of _____, as the Board may authorize, for the purpose of electing directors, and transacting such other business as may properly come before the meeting.

Section 2 - Special Meetings: Special meetings of the shareholders may be called at any time by the Board, the President, or by the holders of twenty-five percent (25%) of the shares then outstanding and entitled to vote.

Section 3 - Place of Meetings: All meetings of shareholders shall be held at the principal office of the Corporation, or at such other places as the board shall designate in the notice of such meetings.

Section 4 - Notice of Meetings: Written or printed notice stating the place, day, and hour of the meeting and, in the case of a special meeting, the purpose of the meeting, shall be delivered personally or by mail not less than ten days, nor more than sixty days, before the date of the meeting. Notice shall be given to each Member of record entitled to vote at the meeting. If mailed, such notice shall be deemed to have been delivered when deposited in the United States Mail with postage paid and addressed to the Member at his address as it appears on the records of the Corporation.

Section 5 - Waiver of Notice: A written waiver of notice signed by a Member, whether before or after a meeting, shall be equivalent to the giving of such notice. Attendance of a Member at a meeting shall constitute a waiver of notice of such meeting, except when the Member attends for the express purpose of objecting, at the beginning of the meeting, to the transaction of any business because the meeting is not lawfully called or convened.

Section 6 - Quorum: Except as otherwise provided by Statute, or the Articles of Incorporation, at all meetings of shareholders of the Corporation, the presence at the commencement of such meetings in person or by proxy of shareholders of record holding a majority of the total number of shares of the Corporation then issued and outstanding and entitled to vote, but in no event less than one-third of the shares entitled to vote at the meeting, shall constitute a quorum for the transaction of any business. If any shareholder leaves after the commencement of a meeting, this shall have no effect on the existence of a quorum, after a quorum has been established at such meeting.

Despite the absence of a quorum at any annual or special meeting of shareholders, the shareholders, by a majority of the votes cast by the holders of shares entitled to vote thereon, may adjourn the meeting. At any such adjourned meeting at which a quorum is present, any business may be transacted at the meeting as originally called as if a quorum had been present.

Section 7 - Voting: Except as otherwise provided by Statute or by the Articles of Incorporation, any corporate action, other than the election of directors, to be taken by vote of the shareholders, shall be authorized by a majority of votes cast at a meeting of shareholders by the holders of shares entitled to vote thereon.

Except as otherwise provided by Statute or by the Articles of Incorporation, at each meeting of shareholders, each holder of record of stock of the Corporation entitled to vote thereat, shall be entitled to one vote for each share of stock registered in his name on the stock transfer books of the corporation.

Each shareholder entitled to vote may do so by proxy; provided, however, that the instrument authorizing such proxy to act shall have been executed in writing by the shareholder himself. No proxy shall be valid after the expiration of eleven months from the date of its execution, unless the person executing it shall have specified therein, the length of time it is to continue in force. Such instrument shall be exhibited to the Secretary at the meeting and shall be filed with the records of the corporation.

Any resolution in writing, signed by all of the shareholders entitled to vote thereon, shall be and constitute action by such shareholders to the effect therein expressed, with the same force and effect as if the same had been duly passed by unanimous vote at a duly called meeting of shareholders and such resolution so signed shall be inserted in the Minute Book of the Corporation under its proper date.

ARTICLE III - BOARD OF DIRECTORS

Section 1 - Number, Election and Term of Office: The number of the directors of the Corporation shall be (____) This number may be increased or decreased by the amendment of these bylaws by the Board but shall in no case be less than ____ director(s). The members of the Board, who need not be shareholders, shall be elected by a majority of the votes cast at a meeting of shareholders entitled to vote in the election. Each director shall hold office until the annual meeting of the shareholders next succeeding his election, and until his successor is elected and qualified, or until his prior death, resignation or removal.

Section 2 - Vacancies: Any vacancy in the Board shall be filled for the unexpired portion of the term by a majority vote of the remaining directors, though less than a quorum, at any regular meeting or special meeting of the Board called for that purpose. Any such director so elected may be replaced by the shareholders at a regular or special meeting of shareholders.

Section 3 - Duties and Powers: The Board shall be responsible for the control and management of the affairs, property and interests of the Corporation, and may exercise all powers of the Corporation, except as limited by statute.

Section 4 - Annual Meetings: An annual meeting of the Board shall be held immediately following the annual meeting of the shareholders, at the place of such annual meeting of shareholders. The Board from time to time, may provide by resolution for the holding of other meetings of the Board, and may fix the time and place thereof.

Section 5 - Special Meetings: Special meetings of the Board shall be held whenever called by the President or by one of the directors, at such time and place as may be specified in the respective notice or waivers of notice thereof.

Section 6 - Notice and Waiver: Notice of any special meeting shall be given at least five days prior thereto by written notice delivered personally, by mail or by telegram to each Director at his address. If mailed, such notice shall be deemed to be delivered when deposited in the United States Mail with postage prepaid. If notice is given by telegram, such notice shall be deemed to be delivered when the telegram is delivered to the telegraph company.

Any Director may waive notice of any meeting, either before, at, or after such meeting, by signing a waiver of notice. The attendance of a Director at a meeting shall constitute a waiver of notice of such meeting and a waiver of any and all objections to the place of such meeting, or the manner in which it has been called or convened, except when a Director states at the beginning of the meeting any objection to the transaction of business because the meeting is not lawfully called or convened.

Section 7 - Chairman: The Board may, at its discretion, elect a Chairman. At all meetings of the Board, the Chairman of the Board, if any and if present, shall preside. If there is no Chairman, or he is absent, then the President shall preside, and in his absence, a Chairman chosen by the directors shall preside.

Section 8 - Quorum and Adjournments: At all meetings of the Board, the presence of a majority of the entire Board shall be necessary and sufficient to constitute a quorum for the transaction of business, except as otherwise provided by law, by the Articles of Incorporation, or by these bylaws. A majority of the directors present at the time and place of any regular or special meeting, although less than a quorum, may adjourn the same from time to time without notice, until a quorum shall be present.

Section 9 - Board Action: At all meetings of the Board, each director present shall have one vote, irrespective of the number of shares of stock, if any, which he may hold. Except as otherwise provided by Statute, the action of a majority of the directors present at any meeting at which a quorum is present shall be the act of the Board. Any action authorized, in writing, by all of the Directors entitled to vote thereon and filed with the minutes of the Corporation shall be the act of the Board with the same force and effect as if the same had been passed by unanimous vote at a duly called meeting of the Board. Any action taken by the Board may be taken without a meeting if agreed to in writing by all members before or after the action is taken and if a record of such action is filed in the minute book.

Section 10 - Telephone Meetings: Directors may participate in meetings of the Board through use of a telephone if such can be arranged so that all Board members can hear all other members. The use of a telephone for participation shall constitute presence in person.

Section 11 - Resignation and Removal: Any director may resign at any time by giving written notice to another Board member, the President or the Secretary of the Corporation. Unless otherwise specified in such written notice, such resignation shall take effect upon receipt thereof by the Board or by such officer, and the acceptance of such resignation shall not be necessary to make it effective. Any director may be removed with or without cause at any time by the affirmative vote of shareholders holding of record in the aggregate at least a majority of the outstanding shares of the Corporation at a special meeting of the shareholders called for that purpose, and may be removed for cause by action of the Board.

Section 12 - Compensation: No stated salary shall be paid to directors, as such for their services, but by resolution of the Board a fixed sum and/or expenses of attendance, if any, may be allowed for attendance at each regular or special meeting of the Board. Nothing herein contained shall be construed to preclude any director from serving the Corporation in any other capacity and receiving compensation therefor.

ARTICLE IV - OFFICERS

Section 1 - Number, Qualification, Election and Term: The officers of the Corporation shall consist of a President, a Secretary, a Treasurer, and such other officers, as the Board may from time to time deem advisable. Any officer may be, but is not required to be, a director of the Corporation. The officers of the Corporation shall be elected by the Board at the regular annual meeting of the Board. Each officer shall hold office until the annual meeting of the Board next succeeding his election, and until his successor shall have been elected and qualified, or until his death, resignation or removal.

Section 2 - Resignation and Removal: Any officer may resign at any time by giving written notice of such resignation to the President or the Secretary of the Corporation or to a member of the Board. Unless otherwise specified in such written notice, such resignation shall take effect upon receipt thereof by the Board member or by such officer, and the acceptance of such resignation shall not be necessary to make it effective. Any officer may be removed, either with or without cause, and a successor elected by a majority vote of the Board at any time.

Section 3 - Vacancies: A vacancy in any office may at any time be filled for the unexpired portion of the term by a majority vote of the Board.

Section 4 - Duties of Officers: Officers of the Corporation shall, unless otherwise provided by the Board, each have such powers and duties as generally pertain to their respective offices as well as such powers and duties as may from time to time be specifically decided by the Board. The President shall be the chief executive officer of the Corporation.

Section 5 - Compensation: The officers of the Corporation shall be entitled to such compensation as the Board shall from time to time determine.

Section 6 - Delegation of Duties: In the absence or disability of any Officer of the Corporation or for any other reason deemed sufficient by the Board of Directors, the Board may delegate his powers or duties to any other Officer or to any other Director.

<u>Section 7 - Shares of Other Corporations</u>: Whenever the Corporation is the holder of shares of any other Corporation, any right or power of the Corporation as such shareholder (including the attendance, acting and voting at shareholders' meetings and execution of waivers, consents, proxies or other instruments) may be exercised on behalf of the Corporation by the President, any Vice President, or such other person as the Board may authorize.

ARTICLE V - COMMITTEES

The Board of Directors may, by resolution, designate an Executive Committee and one or more other committees. Such committees shall have such functions and may exercise such power of the Board of Directors as can be lawfully delegated, and to the extent provided in the resolution or resolutions creating such committee or committees. Meetings of committees may be held without notice at such time and at such place as shall from time to time be determined by the committees. The committees of the corporation shall keep regular minutes of their proceedings, and report these minutes to the Board of Directors when required.

ARTICLE VI - BOOKS, RECORDS AND REPORTS

<u>Section 1 - Annual Report:</u> The Corporation shall send an annual report to the Members of the Corporation not later than _____ months after the close of each fiscal year of the Corporation. Such report shall include a balance sheet as of the close of the fiscal year of the Corporation and a revenue and disbursement statement for the year ending on such closing date. Such financial statements shall be prepared from and in accordance with the books of the Corporation, and in conformity with generally accepted accounting principles applied on a consistent basis.

<u>Section 2 - Permanent Records:</u> The corporation shall keep current and correct records of the accounts, minutes of the meetings and proceedings and membership records of the corporation. Such records shall be kept at the registered office or the principal place of business of the corporation. Any such records shall be in written form or in a form capable of being converted into written form.

<u>Section 3 - Inspection of Corporate Records:</u> Any person who is a Voting Member of the Corporation shall have the right at any reasonable time, and on written demand stating the purpose thereof, to examine and make copies from the relevant books and records of accounts, minutes, and records of the Corporation. Upon the written request of any Voting Member, the Corporation shall mail to such Member a copy of the most recent balance sheet and revenue and disbursement statement.

ARTICLE VII- SHARES OF STOCK

<u>Section 1 - Certificates:</u> Each shareholder of the corporation shall be entitled to have a certificate representing all shares which he or she owns. The form of such certificate shall be adopted by a majority vote of the Board of Directors and shall be signed by the President and Secretary of the Corporation and sealed with the seal of the corporation. No certificate representing shares shall be issued until the full amount of consideration therefore has been paid.

<u>Section 2 - Stock Ledger:</u> The corporation shall maintain a ledger of the stock records of the Corporation. Transfers of shares of the Corporation shall be made on the stock ledger of the Corporation only at the direction of the holder of record upon surrender of the outstanding certificate(s). The Corporation shall be entitled to treat the holder of record of any share or shares as the absolute owner thereof for all purposes and, accordingly, shall not be bound to recognize any legal, equitable or other claim to, or interest in, such share or shares on the part of any other person, whether or not it shall have express or other notice thereof, except as otherwise expressly provided by law.

ARTICLE VIII - DIVIDENDS

Upon approval by the Board of Directors the corporation may pay dividends on its shares in the form of cash, property or additional shares at any time that the corporation is solvent and if such dividends would not render the corporation insolvent.

ARTICLE IX - FISCAL YEAR

The fiscal year of the Corporation shall be the period selected by the Board of Directors as the tax year of the Corporation for federal income tax purposes.

ARTICLE X - CORPORATE SEAL

The Board of Directors may adopt, use and modify a corporate seal. Failure to affix the seal to corporate documents shall not affect the validity of such document.

ARTICLE XI - AMENDMENTS

The Articles of Incorporation may be amended by the Shareholders as provided by _____ statutes. These Bylaws may be altered, amended, or replaced by the Board of Directors; provided, however, that any Bylaws or amendments thereto as adopted by the Board of Directors may be altered, amended, or repealed by vote of the Shareholders. Bylaws adopted by the Members may not be amended or repealed by the Board.

ARTICLE XII - INDEMNIFICATION

Any officer, director or employee of the Corporation shall be indemnified to the full extent allowed by the laws of the State of _____.

Certified to be the Bylaws of the corporation adopted by the Board of Directors on _____, 19____.

_____
Secretary

Banking Resolution of

_____

The undersigned, being the corporate secretary of the above corporation, hereby certifies that on the _____ day of _____, 19____ the Board of Directors of the corporation adopted the following resolution:

RESOLVED that the corporation open bank accounts with _____ _____ and that the officers of the corporation are authorized to take such action as is necessary to open such accounts; that the bank's printed form of resolution is hereby adopted and incorporated into these minutes by reference and shall be placed in the minute book; that any _____ of the following persons shall have signature authority over the account:

_____   _____

_____   _____

and that said resolution has not been modified or rescinded.

Date: _____

_____
Corporate Secretary

(Seal)

Offer to Purchase Stock

Date: _____

To the Board of Directors of

_____

    The undersigned, hereby offers to purchase _____ shares of the
_____ stock of your corporation at a total purchase price of
_____.

                                                    Very truly yours,

                                          _____

- -

Offer to Sell Stock
Pursuant to Sec. 1244 I.R.C.

                                        Date: _____

To: _____

Dear

    The corporation hereby offers to sell to you _____ shares of its common stock at a price of $_____ per share. These shares are issued pursuant to Section 1244 of the Internal Revenue Code,

    Your signature below shall constitute an acceptance of our offer as of the date it is received by the corporation.

                                          Very truly yours,

                                          _____

                                        By:_____

Accepted:

_____

Bill of Sale

The undersigned, in consideration of the issuance of _____ shares of common stock of _____, a _____ corporation, hereby grants, bargains, sells, transfers and delivers unto said corporation the following goods and chattels:

To have and to hold the same forever.

And the undersigned, their heirs, successors and administrators, covenant and warrant that they are the lawful owners of the said goods and chattels and that they are free from all encumbrances. That the undersigned have the right to sell this property and that they will warrant and defend the sale of said property against the lawful claims and demands of all persons.

IN WITNESS whereof the undersigned have executed this Bill of Sale this ____ day of _____19____.

_____

_____

_____

Form **2553**
(Rev. December 1990)

Department of the Treasury
Internal Revenue Service

Election by a Small Business Corporation

(Under section 1362 of the Internal Revenue Code)

▶ For Paperwork Reduction Act Notice, see page 1 of Instructions.
▶ See separate Instructions.

OMB No. 1545-0146

Expires 11-30-93

Notes:
1. This election, to be treated as an "S corporation," can be accepted only if all the tests in General Instruction B are met; all signatures in Parts I and III are originals (no photocopies); and the exact name and address of the corporation and other required form information are provided.
2. Do not file Form 1120S until you are notified that your election is accepted. See General Instruction E.

Part I Election Information

Please Type or Print

Name of corporation (see instructions)	**A** Employer identification number (see instructions)
Number, street, and room or suite no. (If a P.O. box, see instructions.)	**B** Name and telephone number (including area code) of corporate officer or legal representative who may be called for information
City or town, state, and ZIP code	**C** Election is to be effective for tax year beginning (month, day, year)

D Is the corporation the outgrowth or continuation of any form of predecessor? . . ☐ Yes ☐ No   **E** Date of incorporation

If "Yes," state name of predecessor, type of organization, and period of its existence ▶ . . . .

F Check here ▶ ☐ if the corporation has changed its name or address since applying for the employer identification number shown in item A above.   **G** State of incorporation

H If this election takes effect for the first tax year the corporation exists, enter month, day, and year of the **earliest** of the following: (1) date the corporation first had shareholders, (2) date the corporation first had assets, or (3) date the corporation began doing business. ▶

I Selected tax year: Annual return will be filed for tax year ending (month and day) ▶ . . . .
If the tax year ends on any date other than December 31, except for an automatic 52-53-week tax year ending with reference to the month of December, you **must** complete Part II on the back. If the date you enter is the ending date of an automatic 52-53-week tax year, write "52-53-week year" to the right of the date. See Temporary Regulations section 1.441-2T(e)(3).

J Name of each shareholder, person having a community property interest in the corporation's stock, and each tenant in common, joint tenant, and tenant by the entirety. (A husband and wife (and their estates) are counted as one shareholder in determining the number of shareholders without regard to the manner in which the stock is owned.)	K Shareholders' Consent Statement. We, the undersigned shareholders, consent to the corporation's election to be treated as an "S corporation" under section 1362(a). (Shareholders sign and date below.)*		L Stock owned		M Social security number or employer identification number (see instructions)	N Shareholder's tax year ends (month and day)
	Signature	Date	Number of shares	Dates acquired		

*For this election to be valid, the consent of each shareholder, person having a community property interest in the corporation's stock, and each tenant in common, joint tenant, and tenant by the entirety must either appear above or be attached to this form. (See instructions for Column K if continuation sheet or a separate consent statement is needed.)

Under penalties of perjury, I declare that I have examined this election, including accompanying schedules and statements, and to the best of my knowledge and belief, it is true, correct, and complete.

Signature of officer ▶   Title ▶   Date ▶

See Parts II and III on back.   Form **2553**

119

Part II **Selection of Fiscal Tax Year (All corporations using this Part must complete item O and one of items P, Q, or R.)**

O Check the applicable box below to indicate whether the corporation is:

1. ☐ A new corporation adopting the tax year entered in item I, Part I.

2. ☐ An existing corporation retaining the tax year entered in item I, Part I.

3. ☐ An existing corporation changing to the tax year entered in item I, Part I.

P Complete item P if the corporation is using the expeditious approval provisions of Revenue Procedure 87-32, 1987-2 C.B. 396, to request: **(1)** a natural business year (as defined in section 4.01(1) of Rev. Proc. 87-32), or **(2)** a year that satisfies the ownership tax year test in section 4.01(2) of Rev. Proc. 87-32. Check the applicable box below to indicate the representation statement the corporation is making as required under section 4 of Rev. Proc. 87-32.

1. Natural Business Year ► ☐ I represent that the corporation is retaining or changing to a tax year that coincides with its natural business year as defined in section 4.01(1) of Rev. Proc. 87-32 and as verified by its satisfaction of the requirements of section 4.02(1) of Rev. Proc. 87-32. In addition, if the corporation is changing to a natural business year as defined in section 4.01(1), I further represent that such tax year results in less deferral of income to the owners than the corporation's present tax year. I also represent that the corporation is not described in section 3.01(2) of Rev. Proc. 87-32. (See instructions for additional information that must be attached.)

2. Ownership Tax Year ► ☐ I represent that shareholders holding more than half of the shares of the stock (as of the first day of the tax year to which the request relates) of the corporation have the same tax year or are concurrently changing to the tax year that the corporation adopts, retains, or changes to per item I, Part I. I also represent that the corporation is not described in section 3.01(2) of Rev. Proc. 87-32.

Note: *If you do not use item P and the corporation wants a fiscal tax year, complete either item Q or R below. Item Q is used to request a fiscal tax year based on a business purpose and to make a back-up section 444 election. Item R is used to make a regular section 444 election.*

Q Business Purpose—To request a fiscal tax year based on a business purpose, you must check box Q1 and pay a user fee. See instructions for details. You may also check box Q2 and/or box Q3.

1. Check here ► ☐ if the fiscal year entered in item I, Part I, is requested under the provisions of section 6.03 of Rev. Proc. 87-32. Attach to Form 2553 a statement showing the business purpose for the requested fiscal year. See instructions for additional information that must be attached.

2. Check here ► ☐ to show that the corporation intends to make a back-up section 444 election in the event the corporation's business purpose request is not approved by the IRS. (See instructions for more information.)

3. Check here ► ☐ to show that the corporation agrees to adopt or change to a tax year ending December 31 if necessary for the IRS to accept this election for S corporation status in the event: (1) the corporation's business purpose request is not approved and the corporation makes a back-up section 444 election, but is ultimately not qualified to make a section 444 election, or (2) the corporation's business purpose request is not approved and the corporation did not make a back-up section 444 election.

R Section 444 Election—To make a section 444 election, you must check box R1 and you may also check box R2.

1. Check here ► ☐ to show the corporation will make, if qualified, a section 444 election to have the fiscal tax year shown in item I, Part I. To make the election, you must complete **Form 8716**, Election To Have a Tax Year Other Than a Required Tax Year, and either attach it to Form 2553 or file it separately.

2. Check here ► ☐ to show that the corporation agrees to adopt or change to a tax year ending December 31 if necessary for the IRS to accept this election for S corporation status in the event the corporation is ultimately not qualified to make a section 444 election.

Part III **Qualified Subchapter S Trust (QSST) Election Under Section 1361(d)(2)****

Income beneficiary's name and address	Social security number
Trust's name and address	Employer identification number

Date on which stock of the corporation was transferred to the trust (month, day, year) ►

In order for the trust named above to be a QSST and thus a qualifying shareholder of the S corporation for which this Form 2553 is filed, I hereby make the election under section 1361(d)(2). Under penalties of perjury, I certify that the trust meets the definition requirements of section 1361(d)(3) and that all other information provided in Part III is true, correct, and complete.

_____   _____
Signature of income beneficiary or signature and title of legal representative or other qualified person making the election   Date

**Use of Part III to make the QSST election may be made only if stock of the corporation has been transferred to the trust on or before the date on which the corporation makes its election to be an S corporation. The QSST election must be made and filed separately if stock of the corporation is transferred to the trust after the date on which the corporation makes the S election.

★U.S. GPO:1991-518-943/20365

Resolution
of

_____

a _____ Corporation

RESOLVED that the corporation elects "S-Corporation" status for tax purposes under the Internal Revenue Code and that the officers of the corporation are directed to file IRS Form 2553 and to take any further action necessary for the corporation to qualify for S-corporation status.

Shareholders' Consent

The undersigned shareholders being all of the shareholders of the above corporation, a _____ corporation hereby consent to the election of the corporation to obtain S-corporation status

Name and Address of Shareholder	Shares Owned	Date Acquired
_____	_____	_____
_____	_____	_____
_____	_____	_____

Date:_____

_____

_____

_____

_____

_____

WAIVER OF NOTICE OF THE ANNUAL MEETING OF
THE BOARD OF DIRECTORS OF

_____

The undersigned, being all the Directors of the Corporation, hereby agree and consent that an annual meeting of the Board of Directors of the Corporation be held on the ____ day of _____, 19___ at ___ o'clock __m at _____ _____ and do hereby waive all notice whatsoever of such meeting and of any adjournment or adjournments thereof.

We do further agree and consent that any and all lawful business may be transacted at such meeting or at any adjournment or adjournments thereof as may be deemed advisable by the Directors present. Any business transacted at such meeting or at any adjournment or adjournments thereof shall be as valid and legal as if such meeting or adjourned meeting were held after notice.

Date: _____

_____
Director

_____
Director

_____
Director

_____
Director

MINUTES OF THE ANNUAL MEETING OF
THE BOARD OF DIRECTORS OF

_____

The annual meeting of the Board of Directors of the Corporation was held on the date and at the time and place set forth in the written waiver of notice signed by the shareholders, and attached to the minutes of this meeting.

The following were present, being all the directors of the Corporation:

_____   _____
_____   _____

The meeting was called to order and it was moved, seconded and unanimously carried that _____ act as Chairman and that _____ act as Secretary.

The minutes of the last meeting of the Board of Directors which was held on _____, 19___ were read and approved by the Board.

Upon motion duly made, seconded and carried, the following were elected officers for the following year and until their successors are elected and qualify:

President:
Vice President:
Secretary
Treasurer:

There being no further business to come before the meeting, upon motion duly made, seconded and unanimously carried, it was adjourned.

                                        _____
                                        Secretary

Directors:

_____

_____

_____

_____

WAIVER OF NOTICE OF THE ANNUAL MEETING OF
THE SHAREHOLDERS OF

_____

The undersigned, being all the shareholders of the Corporation, hereby agree and consent that an annual meeting of the shareholders of the Corporation be held on the ____ day of _____, 19___ at ___ o'clock __m at _____ _____ and do hereby waive all notice whatsoever of such meeting and of any adjournment or adjournments thereof.

We do further agree and consent that any and all lawful business may be transacted at such meeting or at any adjournment or adjournments thereof. Any business transacted at such meeting or at any adjournment or adjournments thereof shall be as valid and legal as if such meeting or adjourned meeting were held after notice.

Date: _____

_____
Shareholder

_____
Shareholder

_____
Shareholder

_____
Shareholder

MINUTES OF THE ANNUAL MEETING OF
SHAREHOLDERS OF

_____

The annual meeting of Shareholders of the Corporation was held on the date and at the time and place set forth in the written waiver of notice signed by the shareholders, and attached to the minutes of this meeting.

There were present the following shareholders:

Shareholder   No. of Shares

_____   _____
_____   _____
_____   _____
_____   _____

The meeting was called to order and it was moved, seconded and unanimously carried that _____ act as Chairman and that _____ act as Secretary.

A roll call was taken and the Chairman noted that all of the outstanding shares of the Corporation were represented in person or by proxy. Any proxies were attached to these minutes.

The minutes of the last meeting of the shareholders which was held on _____, 19___ were read and approved by the shareholders.

Upon motion duly made, seconded and carried, the following were elected directors for the following year:

_____   _____
_____   _____

There being no further business to come before the meeting, upon motion duly made, seconded and unanimously carried, it was adjourned.

                                    _____
                                    Secretary

Shareholders:

_____

_____

_____

_____

WAIVER OF NOTICE OF SPECIAL MEETING OF
THE BOARD OF DIRECTORS OF

_____

    The undersigned, being all the Directors of the Corporation, hereby agree and consent that a special meeting of the Board of Directors of the Corporation be held on the _____ day of _____, 19___ at ___ o'clock __m at _____ _____ and do hereby waive all notice whatsoever of such meeting and of any adjournment or adjournments thereof.

    The purpose of the meeting is:

    We do further agree and consent that any and all lawful business may be transacted at such meeting or at any adjournment or adjournments thereof as may be deemed advisable by the Directors present. Any business transacted at such meeting or at any adjournment or adjournments thereof shall be as valid and legal as if such meeting or adjourned meeting were held after notice.

Date: _____

_____
Director

_____
Director

_____
Director

_____
Director

MINUTES OF SPECIAL MEETING OF
THE BOARD OF DIRECTORS OF

_____

     A special meeting of the Board of Directors of the Corporation was held on the date and at the time and place set forth in the written waiver of notice signed by the directors, and attached to the minutes of this meeting.

     The following were present, being all the directors of the Corporation:

_____   _____
_____   _____

     The meeting was called to order and it was moved, seconded and unanimously carried that _____ act as Chairman and that _____ act as Secretary.

     The minutes of the last meeting of the Board of Directors which was held on _____, 19___ were read and approved by the Board.

     Upon motion duly made, seconded and carried, the following resolution was adopted:

     There being no further business to come before the meeting, upon motion duly made, seconded and unanimously carried, it was adjourned.

_____
Secretary

Directors:

_____

_____

_____

_____

WAIVER OF NOTICE OF SPECIAL MEETING OF
THE SHAREHOLDERS OF

_____

The undersigned, being all the shareholders of the Corporation, hereby agree and consent that a special meeting of the shareholders of the Corporation be held on the ____ day of _____, 19___ at ___ o'clock __m at _____ _____ and do hereby waive all notice whatsoever of such meeting and of any adjournment or adjournments thereof.

The purpose of the meeting is

We do further agree and consent that any and all lawful business may be transacted at such meeting or at any adjournment or adjournments thereof. Any business transacted at such meeting or at any adjournment or adjournments thereof shall be as valid and legal as if such meeting or adjourned meeting were held after notice.

Date: _____

_____
Shareholder

_____
Shareholder

_____
Shareholder

_____
Shareholder

MINUTES OF SPECIAL MEETING OF
SHAREHOLDERS OF

_____

A special meeting of Shareholders of the Corporation was held on the date and at the time and place set forth in the written waiver of notice signed by the shareholders, and attached to the minutes of this meeting.

There were present the following shareholders:

Shareholder   No. of Shares
_____   _____
_____   _____
_____   _____
_____   _____

The meeting was called to order and it was moved, seconded and unanimously carried that _____ act as Chairman and that _____ act as Secretary.

A roll call was taken and the Chairman noted that all of the outstanding shares of the Corporation were represented in person or by proxy. Any proxies were attached to these minutes.

The minutes of the last meeting of the shareholders which was held on _____, 19___ were read and approved by the shareholders.

Upon motion duly made, seconded and carried, the following resolution was adopted:

There being no further business to come before the meeting, upon motion duly made, seconded and unanimously carried, it was adjourned.

_____
Secretary

Shareholders:

_____

_____

_____

_____

Change of Registered Agent and/or Registered Office

1. The name of the corporation is:

2. The street address of the current registered office is:

3. The new address of the registered office is to be:

4. The current registered agent is:

5. The new registered agent is:

6. The street address of the registered office and the street address of the business address of the registered agent are identical.

7. Such change was authorized by resolution duly adopted by the Board of Directors of the corporation or by an officer of the corporation so authorized by the board of directors.

_____
Secretary

Having been named as registered agent and to accept service of process for the above stated corporation at the place designated in this certificate, I hereby accept the appointment as registered agent and agree to act in this capacity. I further agree to comply with the provisions of all statutes relating to the proper and complete performance of my duties, and am familiar with and accept the obligations of my position as registered agent.

_____
Registered Agent

Stock Ledger

Transfer of Shares

Certificates Issued

Cert. No.	No. of Shares	Date of Acquisition	Shareholder Name and Address	From Whom Transferred	Amount Paid	Date of Transfer	To Whom Transferred	Cert. No. Surrendered	No. of Shares Transferred	Cert. No.

Received Cert. No._____
No. of shares
New certificates issued:
Cert. No.   No. of Shares
_____   _____
_____   _____

☐ Transferred from:
_____

Date: _____
Original   Original   No. of Shares
Cert. No.   No. Shares   Transferred
_____   _____   _____

☐ Original issue
Documentary stamp tax paid:
$ _____
(Attach stamps to this stub.)

Certificate No._____
No. of shares _____
Dated _____
Issued to:
_____
_____

Received Cert. No._____
No. of shares
New certificates issued:
Cert. No.   No. of Shares
_____   _____
_____   _____

☐ Transferred from:
_____

Date: _____
Original   Original   No. of Shares
Cert. No.   No. Shares   Transferred
_____   _____   _____

☐ Original issue
Documentary stamp tax paid:
$ _____
(Attach stamps to this stub.)

Certificate No._____
No. of shares _____
Dated _____
Issued to:
_____
_____

Received Cert. No._____
No. of shares
New certificates issued:
Cert. No.   No. of Shares
_____   _____
_____   _____

☐ Transferred from:
_____

Date: _____
Original   Original   No. of Shares
Cert. No.   No. Shares   Transferred
_____   _____   _____

☐ Original issue
Documentary stamp tax paid:
$ _____
(Attach stamps to this stub.)

Certificate No._____
No. of shares _____
Dated _____
Issued to:
_____
_____

Form v. Stock Certificate

Shares

Certificate No.

The shares represented by this certificate have not been registered under state or federal securities laws. Therefore, they may not be transferred until the corporation determines that such transfer will not adversely affect the exemptions relied upon.

Organized under the laws of the

This certifies that

is the holder of record of

_____ shares of _____ stock of

transferable only on the books of the corporation by the holder hereof in person or by Attorney upon surrender of this certificate properly endorsed.

In witness whereof, the said corporation has caused this certificate to be signed by its duly authorized officers and its corporate seal to be hereto affixed this _____ day of _____, 19____.

For value received, _____ hereby sell, assign and transfer unto _____

_____,

_____ shares

represented by this certificate and do hereby irrevocably constitute and appoint

_____ attorney to transfer the said shares on

the books of the corporation with full power of substitution in the premises.

Dated _____

Witness:

_____

_____

Index

Sphinx Publishing Presents

Self-Help Law Books

Laymen's Guides to The Law

Neighbor
vs.
Neighbor

Legal Rights of Neighbors in Dispute

Mark Warda
Attorney at Law

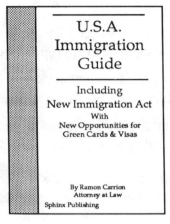

U.S.A.
Immigration
Guide

Including
New Immigration Act
With
New Opportunities for
Green Cards & Visas

By Ramon Carrion
Attorney at Law

Sphinx Publishing

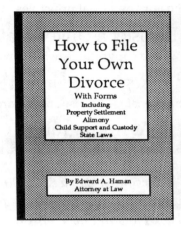

How to File
Your Own
Divorce
With Forms
Including
Property Settlement
Alimony
Child Support and Custody
State Laws

By Edward A. Haman
Attorney at Law

How to Form
Your Own
Corporation
With Forms
Including
State-by-State Laws
Forms for every state

By Keleen Wilber & Arthur Sartorius
Attorney at Law

What our customers say about our books:

"It couldn't be more clear for the lay person." R.D.

"I want you to know I really appreciate your book. It has saved me a lot of time and money." L.T.

"Your real estate contracts book has saved me nearly $12,000.00 in closing costs over the past year." A.B.

"...many of the legal questions that I have had over the years were answered clearly and concisely through your plain English interpretation of the law." C.E.H.

"If there weren't people out there like you I'd be lost. You have the best books of this type out there." S.B.

"...your forms and directions are easy to follow..." C.V.M.

Sphinx titles are available directly from the publisher or from independent book stores and chain stores such as B. Dalton, Bookland, Bookstop, and Waldenbooks.

Our National titles are valid in all 50 States

Popular Legal Topics

- **How to File Your Own Bankruptcy** (or How to Avoid It) By Edward Haman, Atty., 2nd Ed., $19.95
  Explains how to evaluate your financial situation, consider the options and file your own bankruptcy, if necessary.

- **Debtors' Rights, A Legal Self-Help Guide** By Gudrun Nickel, Atty., $12.95
  Explains the legal rights of people who owe money in all types of matters.

- **Neighbor vs. Neighbor, Legal Rights of Neighbors in Dispute** By Mark Warda, Atty., $12.95
  Explains all the laws and legal principles involved in neighbor disputes. Includes over 400 true cases.

- **How to Register a United States Copyright** By Mark Warda, Atty., 3rd Ed., $14.95
  Explains what a copyright is, what can and cannot be copyrighted, benefits of registration and more.

- **How to Register a United States Trademark** By Mark Warda, Atty., 3rd Ed., $14.95
  Explains benefits of registration, searching and choosing a trademark, and the types of registration.

- **U. S. A. Immigration Guide** By Ramon Carrion, Atty., $19.95.
  Explains the immigration process including new opportunities for Green Cards & Visas.

> *"Filers must pay a $120.00 court fee, but there's no legal requirements to have an attorney. Rather, do-it-yourselfers can turn to books, such as $19.95 paperback How to File Your Own Bankruptcy (or How to Avoid It) from Sphinx Publishing in Clearwater, Fl."*
> Business Week

How to File Your Own Bankruptcy (or How to Avoid It)

With Forms

Includes
Chapter 7 (Discharge of Debts)
Chapter 13 (Payment Plan)

Sphinx Publishing

- **How to File Your Own Divorce** By Edward Haman, Atty., $19.95
  Explains all aspects of filing for a divorce, including alimony and child support. Includes laws of all 50 states.

- **How to Form Your Own Corporation** By Kelsea Wilber & Arthur Sartorious, Attys., $19.95
  Explains how to register a for profit corporation, including corporate minutes.

- **How to Write Your Own Premarital Agreement** By Edward Haman, Atty., $19.95
  Provides instructions and forms for writing a premarital agreement

- **How to Write Your Own Partnership Agreement** By Edward Haman, Atty., $19.95
  Explains how to write a sound partnership agreement.

- **The Power of Attorney Handbook** By Edward Haman, Atty., $19.95
  Explains an official way to give someone else authorization to handle particular transactions for specific amounts of time.

- **How to Negotiate Real Estate Contracts** By Mark Warda, Atty., $14.95
  Explains in simple language the type of clauses used and why different versions are better for buyers or sellers.

- **How to Negotiate Real Estate Leases** By Mark Warda, Atty., $14.95
  Explains in simple language each clause used in leases and which version is best for land lords or tenants.

> *"Debtors' Rights . . . a very good reference and source of information for debtor decision-making."*
> George Hampton, Booklist